MW01008736

THE UNDERCOMMONS
FUGITIVE PLANNING & BLACK STUDY

STEFANO HARNEY & FRED MOTEN

The Undercommons: Fugitive Planning & Black Study
Stefano Harney and Fred Moten

ISBN 978-1-57027-267-7

Cover & book design by fFurious, Singapore (www.ffurious.com)

Copyedited by Erik Empson

Released by Minor Compositions 2013
Wivenhoe / New York / Port Watson

Minor Compositions is a series of interventions & provocations drawing from
autonomous politics, avant-garde aesthetics, and the revolutions of everyday life.

Minor Compositions is an imprint of Autonomedia
www.minorcompositions.info | minorcompositions@gmail.com

Distributed by Autonomedia
PO Box 568 Williamsburgh Station
Brooklyn, NY 11211

www.autonomedia.org
info@autonomedia.org

Some of the chapters were published in earlier form by Duke University Press,
Social Text, South Atlantic Quarterly, and *E-flux.* The authors would like to
thank the editors and publishers.

For our mentor,
Martin L. Kilson

CONTENTS

THE WILD BEYOND:
WITH AND FOR
THE UNDERCOMMONS

JACK HALBERSTAM

It ends with love, exchange, fellowship. It ends as it begins, in motion, in between various modes of being and belonging, and on the way to new economies of giving, taking, being with and for and it ends with a ride in a Buick Skylark on the way to another place altogether. Surprising, perhaps, after we have engaged dispossession, debt, dislocation and violence. But not surprising when you have understood that the projects of "fugitive planning and black study" are mostly about reaching out to find connection; they are about making common cause with the brokenness of being, a brokenness, I would venture to say, that is also blackness, that remains blackness, and will, despite all, remain broken because this book is not a prescription for repair.

If we do not seek to fix what has been broken, then what? How do we resolve to live with brokenness, with being broke, which is also what Moten and Harney call "debt." Well, given that debt is sometimes a history of giving, at other times a history of taking, at all times a history of capitalism and given that debt also signifies a promise of ownership but never delivers on that promise, we have to understand that debt is something that cannot be paid off. Debt, as Harney puts it, presumes a kind of individualized relation to a naturalized economy that is predicated upon exploitation. Can we have, he asks, another sense of what is owed that does not presume a nexus of activities like recognition and acknowledgement, payment and gratitude. Can debt "become a principle of elaboration"?

Moten links economic debt to the brokenness of being in the interview with Stevphen Shukaitis; he acknowledges that some debts should be paid, and that much is owed especially to black people by white people, and yet, he says: "I also know that what it is that is supposed to be repaired is irreparable. It can't be repaired. The only thing we can do is tear this shit down completely and build something new." The undercommons do not come to pay their debts, to repair what has been broken, to fix what has come undone.

If you want to know what the undercommons wants, what Moten and Harney want, what black people, indigenous peoples, queers and poor people want, what we (the "we" who cohabit in the space of the undercommons) want, it is this – we cannot be satisfied with the recognition and acknowledgement generated by the very system that denies a) that anything was ever broken and b) that we deserved to be the broken part; so we refuse to ask for recognition and instead we want to take apart, dismantle, tear down the structure that, right now, limits our ability to find each other, to see beyond it and to access the places that we know lie outside its walls. We cannot say what new structures will replace the ones we live with yet, because once we have torn shit down, we will inevitably see more and see differently and feel a new sense of wanting and being and becoming. What we want after "the break" will be different from what we think we want before the break and both are necessarily different from the desire that issues from being in the break.

refusal of recognition

Let's come at this by another path. In the melancholic and visionary 2009 film version of Maurice Sandak's *Where The Wild Things Are* (1963), Max, the small seeker who leaves his room, his home, his family to find the wild beyond, finds a world of lost and lonely beasts and they promptly make him their king. Max is the first king the wild things have had whom they did not eat and who did not, in turn, try to eat them; and the beasts are the first grown things that Max has met who want his opinion, his judgment, his rule. Max's power is that he is small while they are big; he promises the beasts that he has no plans to eat them and this is more than anyone has ever promised them. He promises that he will find ways through and around and will "slip through cracks" and re-crack the cracks if they fill up. He promises to keep sadness at bay and to make a world with the wild creatures that "roared their terrible roars and gnashed their terrible teeth and rolled their terrible eyes and showed their terrible claws." That Max fails to make the wild things happy or to save them or to make a world with them is less important than the fact that he found them and he recognized in them the end of something and potentially the path to an alternative to his world. The wild things were not the utopian creatures of fairy tales, they were the rejected and lost subjects of the world Max had left behind and, because he shuttles between the Oedipal land where his mother rules and the ruined world of the wild, he knows the parameters of the real – he sees what is included and what is left out and he is now able to set sail for another place, a place that is neither the home he left nor the home to which he wants to return.

Moten and Harney want to gesture to another place, a wild place that is not simply the left over space that limns real and regulated zones of polite society; rather, it is a wild place that continuously produces its own unregulated wildness. The zone we enter through Moten and Harney is ongoing and exists in the present and, as Harney puts it, "some kind of demand was already being enacted, fulfilled in the call itself." While describing the London Riots of 2011, Harney suggests that the riots and insurrections do not separate out "the request, the demand and the call" – rather, they enact the one in the other: "I think the call, in the way I would understand it, the call, as in the call and response, the response is already there before the call goes out. You're already in something." *You are already in it.* For Moten too, you are always already in the thing that you call for and that calls you. What's more, the call is always a call to dis-order and this disorder or wildness shows up in many places: in jazz, in improvisation, in noise. The disordered sounds that we refer to as cacophony will always be cast as "extra-musical," as Moten puts it, precisely because we hear something in them that reminds us that our desire for harmony is arbitrary and in another world, harmony would sound incomprehensible. Listening to cacophony and noise tells us that there is a wild beyond to the structures we inhabit and that inhabit us.

And when we are called to this other place, the wild beyond, "beyond the beyond" in Moten and Harney's apt terminology, we have to give ourselves over to a certain kind of craziness. Moten reminds us that even as Fanon took an anti-colonial stance, he knew that it "looks crazy" but, Fanon, as a psychiatrist, also knew *not* to accept this organic division between the rational and the crazy and he knew that it would be crazy for him not to take that stance in a world that had assigned to him the role of the unreal, the primitive and the wild. Fanon, according to Moten, wants not the end of colonialism but the end of the standpoint from which colonialism makes sense. In order to bring colonialism to an end then, one does not speak truth to power, one has to inhabit the crazy, nonsensical, ranting language of the other, the other who has been rendered a nonentity by colonialism. Indeed, blackness, for Moten and Harney by way of Fanon, is the willingness to be in the space that has been abandoned by colonialism, by rule, by order. Moten takes us there, saying of Fanon finally: "Eventually, I believe, he comes to believe in the world, which is to say the other world, where we inhabit and maybe even cultivate this absence, this place which shows up here and now, in the sovereign's space and time, as absence, darkness, death, things which are not (as John Donne would say)."

The path to the wild beyond is paved with refusal. In *The Undercommons* if we begin anywhere, we begin with the right to refuse what has been refused to you. Citing Gayatri Spivak, Moten and Harney call this refusal the "first right" and it is a game-changing kind of refusal in that it signals the refusal of the choices as offered. We can understand this refusal in terms that Chandan Reddy lays out in *Freedom With Violence* (2011) – for Reddy, gay marriage is the option that cannot be opposed in the ballot box. While we can circulate multiple critiques of gay marriage in terms of its institutionalization of intimacy, when you arrive at the ballot box, pen in hand, you only get to check "yes" or "no" and the no, in this case, could be more damning than the yes. And so, you must refuse the choice as offered.

Moten and Harney also study what it would mean to refuse what they term "the call to order." And what would it mean, furthermore, to refuse to call others to order, to refuse interpellation and the re-instantiation of the law. When we refuse, Moten and Harney suggest, we create dissonance and more importantly, we allow dissonance to continue – when we enter a classroom and we refuse to call it to order, we are allowing study to continue, dissonant study perhaps, disorganized study, but study that precedes our call and will continue after we have left the room. Or, when we listen to music, we must refuse the idea that music happens only when the musician enters and picks up an instrument; music is also the anticipation of the performance and the noises of appreciation it generates and the speaking that happens through and around it, making it and loving it, being in it while listening. And so, when we refuse the call to order – the teacher picking up the book, the conductor raising his baton, the speaker asking for silence, the torturer tightening the noose – we refuse order as the distinction between noise and music, chatter and knowledge, pain and truth.

like Burkean parlor

These kinds of examples get to the heart of Moten and Harney's world of the undercommons – the undercommons is not a realm where we rebel and we create critique; it is not a place where we "take arms against a sea of troubles/and by opposing end them." The undercommons is a space and time which is always here. Our goal – and the "we" is always the right mode of address here – is not to end the troubles but to end the world that created those particular troubles as the ones that must be opposed. Moten and Harney refuse the logic that stages refusal as inactivity, as the absence of a plan and as a mode of stalling real politics. Moten and Harney tell us to listen to the noise we make and to refuse the offers we receive to shape that noise into "music."

In the essay that many people already know best from this volume, "The University and the Undercommons," Moten and Harney come closest to explaining their mission. Refusing to be for or against the university and in fact marking the critical academic as the player who holds the "for and against" logic in place, Moten and Harney lead us to the "Undercommons of the Enlightenment" where subversive intellectuals engage both the university and fugitivity: "where the work gets done, where the work gets subverted, where the revolution is still black, still strong." The subversive intellectual, we learn, is unprofessional, uncollegial, passionate and disloyal. The subversive intellectual is neither trying to extend the university nor change the university, the subversive intellectual is not toiling in misery and from this place of misery articulating a "general antagonism." In fact, the subversive intellectual enjoys the ride and wants it to be faster and wilder; she does not want a room of his or her own, she wants to be in the world, in the world with others and making the world anew. Moten insists: "Like Deleuze. I believe in the world and want to be in it. I want to be in it all the way to the end of it because I believe in another world in the world and I want to be in *that*. And I plan to stay a believer, like Curtis Mayfield. But that's beyond me, and even beyond me and Stefano, and out into the world, the other thing, the other world, the joyful noise of the scattered, scatted eschaton, the undercommon refusal of the academy of misery."

The mission then for the denizens of the undercommons is to recognize that when you seek to make things better, you are not just doing it for the Other, you must also be doing it for yourself. While men may think they are being "sensitive" by turning to feminism, while white people may think they are being right on by opposing racism, no one will really be able to embrace the mission of tearing "this shit down" until they realize that the structures they oppose are not only bad for some of us, they are bad for all of us. Gender hierarchies are bad for men as well as women and they are really bad for the rest of us. Racial hierarchies are not rational and ordered, they are chaotic and nonsensical and must be opposed by precisely all those who benefit in any way from them. Or, as Moten puts it: "The coalition emerges out of your recognition that it's fucked up for you, in the same way that we've already recognized that it's fucked up for us. I don't need your help. I just need you to recognize that this shit is killing you, too, however much more softly, you stupid motherfucker, you know?"

The coalition unites us in the recognition that we must change things or die. All of us. We must all change the things that are fucked up and change cannot come in the form that we think of as "revolutionary"

– not as a masculinist surge or an armed confrontation. Revolution will come in a form we cannot yet imagine. Moten and Harney propose that we prepare now for what will come by entering into *study*. Study, a mode of thinking with others separate from the thinking that the institution requires of you, prepares us to be embedded in what Harney calls "the with and for" and allows you to spend less time antagonized and antagonizing.

Like all world-making and all world-shattering encounters, when you enter this book and learn how to be with and for, in coalition, and on the way to the place we are already making, you will also feel fear, trepidation, concern, and disorientation. The disorientation, Moten and Harney will tell you is not just unfortunate, it is necessary because you will no longer be in one location moving forward to another, instead you will already be part of "the "movement of things" and on the way to this "outlawed social life of nothing." The movement of things can be felt and touched and exists in language and in fantasy, it is flight, it is motion, it is fugitivity itself. Fugitivity is not only escape, "exit" as Paolo Virno might put it, or "exodus" in the terms offered by Hardt and Negri, fugitivity is being separate from settling. It is a being in motion that has learned that "organizations are obstacles to organising ourselves" (The Invisible Committee in *The Coming Insurrection*) and that there are spaces and modalities that exist separate from the logical, logistical, the housed and the positioned. Moten and Harney call this mode a "being together in homelessness" which does not idealize homelessness nor merely metaphorize it. Homelessness is the state of dispossession that we seek and that we embrace: "Can this being together in homelessness, this interplay of the refusal of what has been refused, this undercommon appositionality, be a place from which emerges neither self-consciousness nor knowledge of the other but an improvisation that proceeds from somewhere on the other side of an unasked question?" I think this is what Jay-Z and Kanye West (another collaborative unit of study) call "no church in the wild."

For Fred Moten and Stefano Harney, we must make common cause with those desires and (non) positions that seem crazy and unimaginable: we must, on behalf of this alignment, refuse that which was first refused to us and in this refusal reshape desire, reorient hope, reimagine possibility and do so separate from the fantasies nestled into rights and respectability. Instead, our fantasies must come from what Moten and Harney citing Frank B. Wilderson III call "the hold": "And so it is we remain in the hold, in the break, as if entering again and again the broken world, to trace the visionary company and join it." The hold here is the hold in the slave ship but it is also the hold that we have on reality and fantasy, the hold they have on us and the hold we decide to forego on the other, preferring instead to touch, to be with, to love. If there is no church in the wild, if there is study rather than knowledge production, if there is a way of being together in brokenness, if there is an undercommons, then we must all find our way to it. And it will not be there where the wild things are, it will be a place where refuge is not necessary and you will find that you were already in it all along.

Love,

J

REFERENCES

The Invisible Committee, *The Coming Insurrection* (NY: Semiotexte, 2009).

Chandan Reddy, *Freedom With Violence: Race, Sexuality and the US State* (Durham, NC: Duke UP, 2011).

Maurice Sendak, *Where the Wild Things Are* (NY: Harper Collins, 1988).

POLITICS SURROUNDED

In Michael Parenti's classic anti-imperial analysis of Hollywood movies, he points to the 'upside down' way that the 'make-believe media' portrays colonial settlement. In films like *Drums Along the Mohawk* (1939) or *Shaka Zulu* (1987), the settler is portrayed as surrounded by 'natives,' inverting, in Parenti's view, the role of aggressor so that colonialism is made to look like self-defense. Indeed, aggression and self-defense are reversed in these movies, but the image of a surrounded fort is not false. Instead, the false image is what emerges when a critique of militarised life is predicated on the forgetting of the life that surrounds it. The fort really was surrounded, is besieged by what still surrounds it, the common beyond and beneath – before and before – enclosure. The surround antagonises the laager in its midst while disturbing that facts on the ground with some outlaw planning.

Our task is the self-defense of the surround in the face of repeated, targeted dispossessions through the settler's armed incursion. And while acquisitive violence occasions this self-defense, it is recourse to self-possession in the face of dispossession (recourse, in other words, to politics) that represents the real danger. Politics is an ongoing attack on the common – the general and generative antagonism – from within the surround.

Consider the Black Panther Party for Self-Defense, first theorists of the revolution of the surround, the black before and before, the already and the forthcoming. Their twinned commitment to revolution and self-defense emerged from the recognition that the preservation of black social life is articulated in and with the violence of innovation. This is not a contradiction if the new thing, always calling for itself, already lives around and below the forts, the police stations, the patrolled highways and the prison towers. The Panthers theorized revolution without politics, which is to say revolution with neither a subject nor a principle of decision. Against the law because they were generating law, they practiced an ongoing planning to be possessed, hopelessly and optimistically and incessantly indebted, given to unfinished, contrapuntal study of, and in, the common wealth, poverty and the blackness of the surround.

The self-defense of revolution is confronted not only by the brutalities but also by the false image of enclosure. The hard materiality of the unreal convinces us that we are surrounded, that we must take possession of ourselves, correct ourselves, remain in the emergency, on a permanent footing, settled, determined, protecting nothing but an illusory right to what we do not have, which the settler takes for and as the commons. But in the moment of right/s the commons is already gone in the movement to and of the common that surrounds it and its enclosure. What's left is politics but even the politics of the commons, of the resistance to enclosure, can only be a politics of ends, a rectitude aimed at the regulatory end of the common. And even when the election that was won turns out to have been lost, and the bomb detonates and/or fails to detonate, the common perseveres as if a kind of elsewhere, here, around, on the ground, surrounding hallucinogenic facts. Meanwhile, politics soldiers on, claiming to defend what it has not enclosed, enclosing what it cannot defend but only endanger.

The settler, having settled for politics, arms himself in the name of civilisation while critique initiates the self-defense of those of us who see hostility in the civil union of settlement and enclosure. We say, rightly, if our critical eyes are sharp enough, that it's evil and uncool to have a place in the sun in the dirty thinness of this atmosphere; that house the sheriff was building is in the heart of a fallout zone. And if our eyes carry sharpness farther out we trail the police so we can put them on trial. Having looked for politics in order to avoid it, we move next to each other, so we can be beside ourselves, because we like the nightlife which ain't no good life. Critique lets us know that politics is radioactive, but politics is the radiation of critique. So it matters how long we have to do it, how long we have to be exposed to the lethal effects of its anti-social energy. Critique endangers the sociality it is supposed to defend, not because it might turn inward to damage politics but because it would turn to politics and then turn outward, from the fort to the surround, were it not for preservation, which is given in celebration of what we defend, the sociopoetic force we wrap tightly round us, since we are poor. Taking down our critique, our own positions, our fortifications, is self-defense alloyed with self-preservation. That takedown comes in movement, as a shawl, the armor of flight. We run looking for a weapon and keep running looking to drop it. And we can drop it, because however armed, however hard, the enemy we face is also illusory.

Uncut devotion to the critique of this illusion makes us delusional. In the trick of politics we are insufficient, scarce, waiting in pockets of resistance, in stairwells, in alleys, in vain. The false image and its critique threaten the common with democracy, which is only ever to come, so that one day, which is only never to come, we will be more than what we are. But we already are. We're already here, moving. We've been around. We're more than politics, more than settled, more than democratic. We surround democracy's false image in order to unsettle it. Every time it tries to enclose us in a decision, we're undecided. Every time it tries to represent our will, we're unwilling. Every time it tries to take root, we're gone (because we're already here, moving). We ask and we tell and we cast the spell that we are under, which tells us what to do and how we shall be moved, here, where we dance the war of apposition. We're in a trance that's under and around us. We move through it and it moves with us, out beyond the settlements, out beyond the redevelopment, where black night is falling, where we hate to be alone, back inside to sleep till morning, drink till morning, plan till morning, as the common embrace, right inside, and around, in the surround.

In the clear, critical light of day, illusory administrators whisper of our need for institutions, and all institutions are political, and all politics is correctional, so it seems we need correctional institutions in the common, settling it, correcting us. But we won't stand corrected. Moreover, incorrect as we are there's nothing wrong with us. We don't want to be correct and we won't be corrected. Politics proposes to make us better, but we were good already in the mutual debt that can never be made good. We owe it to each other to falsify the institution, to make politics incorrect, to give the lie to our own determination. We owe each other the indeterminate. We owe each other everything.

An abdication of political responsibility? OK. Whatever. We're just anti-politically romantic about actually existing social life. We aren't responsible for politics. We are the general antagonism to politics looming outside every attempt to politicise, every imposition of self-governance, every sovereign decision and its degraded miniature, every emergent state and home sweet home. We are disruption and consent to disruption. We preserve upheaval. Sent to fulfill by abolishing, to renew by unsettling, to open the enclosure whose immeasurable venality is inversely proportionate to its actual area, we got politics surrounded. We cannot represent ourselves. We can't be represented.

Rancière's politics

THE UNIVERSITY AND
THE UNDERCOMMONS

Philosophy thus traditionally practices a critique of knowledge which is simultaneously a denegation of knowledge (i.e., of the class struggle). Its position can be described as an irony with regard to knowledge, which it puts into question without ever touching its foundations. The questioning of knowledge in philosophy always ends in its restoration: a movement great philosophers consistently expose in each other.

Jacques Rancière, *On the Theory of Ideology*
– *Althusser's Politics*

I am a black man number one, because I am against what they have done and are still doing to us; and number two, I have something to say about the new society to be built because I have
a tremendous part in that which they have sought to discredit.

C. L. R. James, *C. L. R. James: His Life and Work*

THE ONLY POSSIBLE RELATIONSHIP TO THE UNIVERSITY TODAY IS A CRIMINAL ONE

"To the university I'll steal, and there I'll steal," to borrow from Pistol at the end of Henry V, as he would surely borrow from us. This is the only possible relationship to the American university today. This may be true of universities everywhere. It may have to be true of the university in general. But certainly, this much is true in the United States: it cannot be denied that the university is a place of refuge, and it cannot be accepted that the university is a place of enlightenment. In the face of these conditions one can only sneak into the university and steal what one can. To abuse its hospitality, to spite its mission, to join its refugee colony, its gypsy encampment, to be in but not of – this is the path of the subversive intellectual in the modern university.

Worry about the university. This is the injunction today in the United States, one with a long history. Call for its restoration like Harold Bloom or Stanley Fish or Gerald Graff. Call for its reform like Derek Bok or Bill Readings or Cary Nelson. Call out to it as it calls to you. But for the subversive intellectual, all of this goes on upstairs, in polite company, among the rational men. After all, the subversive intellectual came under false pretenses, with bad documents, out of love. Her labor is as necessary as it is unwelcome. The university needs what she bears but cannot bear what she brings. And on top of all that, she disappears. She disappears into the underground, the downlow lowdown maroon community of the university, into the *undercommons of enlightenment*, where the work gets done, where the work gets subverted, where the revolution is still black, still strong.

What is that work and what is its social capacity for both reproducing the university and producing fugitivity? If one were to say teaching, one would be performing the work of the university. Teaching is merely a profession and an operation of that onto-/auto-encyclopedic circle of the state" that Jacques Derrida calls the Universitas. But it is useful to invoke this operation to glimpse the hole in the fence where labor enters, to glimpse its hiring hall, its night quarters. The university needs teaching labor, despite itself, or as itself, self-identical with and thereby erased by it. It is not teaching that holds this social capacity, but something that produces the not visible other side of teaching, a thinking through the skin of teaching toward a collective orientation to the knowledge object as future project, and a commitment to what we want to call the prophetic organization. But it is teaching that brings us in. Before there are grants, research, conferences, books, and journals there is the experience of being taught and of teaching. Before the research post with no teaching, before the graduate students to mark the exams, before the string of sabbaticals, before the permanent reduction in teaching load, the appointment to run the Center, the consignment of pedagogy to a discipline called education, before the course designed to be a new book, teaching happened.

The moment of teaching for food is therefore often mistakenly taken to be a stage, as if eventually one should not teach for food. If the stage persists, there is a social pathology in the university. But if the teaching is successfully passed on, the stage is surpassed, and teaching is consigned to those who are known to remain in the stage, the socio-pathological labor of the university. Kant interestingly calls such a stage "self-incurred minority." He tries to contrast it with having the "determination and courage to use one's intelligence without being guided by another." "Have the courage to use your own intelligence." But what would it mean if teaching or rather what we might call "the beyond of teaching" is precisely what one is asked to get beyond, to stop taking sustenance? And what of those minorities who refuse, the tribe of moles who will not come back from beyond (that which is beyond "the beyond of teaching"), as if they will not be subjects, as if they want to think as objects, as minority? Certainly, the perfect subjects of communication, those successfully beyond teaching, will see them as waste. But their collective labor will always call into question who truly is taking the orders of the enlightenment. The waste lives for those moments beyond teaching when you give away the unexpected beautiful phrase – unexpected, no one has asked, beautiful, it will never come back. Is being the biopower of the enlightenment truly better than this?

Perhaps the biopower of the enlightenment knows this, or perhaps it is just reacting to the objecthood of this labor as it must. But even as it depends on these moles, these refugees, it will call them uncollegial, impractical, naive, unprofessional. And one may be given one last chance to be pragmatic – why steal when one can have it all, they will ask. But if one hides from this interpellation, neither agrees nor disagrees but goes with hands full into the underground of the university, into the Undercommons – this will be regarded as theft, as a criminal act. And it is at the same time, the only possible act.

In that undercommons of the university one can see that it is not a matter of teaching versus research or even the beyond of teaching versus the individualisation of research. To enter this space is to inhabit the ruptural and enraptured disclosure of the commons that fugitive enlightenment enacts, the criminal, matricidal, queer, in the cistern, on the stroll of the stolen life, the life stolen by enlightenment and stolen back, where the commons give refuge, where the refuge gives commons. What the beyond of teaching is really about is not finishing oneself, not passing, not completing; it's about allowing subjectivity to be unlawfully overcome by others, a radical passion and passivity such that one becomes unfit for subjection, because one does not possess the kind of agency that can hold the regulatory forces of subjecthood, and one cannot initiate the auto-interpellative torque that biopower subjection requires and rewards. It is not so much the teaching as it is the prophecy in the organization of the act of teaching. The prophecy that predicts its own organization and has therefore passed, as commons, and the prophecy that exceeds its own organization and therefore as yet can only be organized. Against the prophetic organization of the undercommons is arrayed its own deadening labor for the university, and beyond that, the negligence of professionalization, and the professionalization of the critical academic. The undercommons is therefore always an unsafe neighborhood.

As Fredric Jameson reminds us, the university depends upon "Enlightenment-type critiques and demystification of belief and committed ideology, in order to clear the ground for unobstructed planning and 'development.'" This is the weakness of the university, the lapse in its homeland security. It needs labor power for this "enlightenment-type critique," but, somehow, labor always escapes.

The premature subjects of the undercommons took the call seriously, or had to be serious about the call. They were not clear about planning, too mystical, too full of belief. And yet this labor force cannot reproduce itself, it must be reproduced. The university works for the day when it will be able to rid itself, like capital in general, of the trouble of labor. It will then be able to reproduce a labor force that understands itself as not only unnecessary but dangerous to the development of capitalism. Much pedagogy and scholarship is already dedicated in this direction. Students must come to see themselves as the problem, which, counter to the complaints of restorationist critics of the university, is precisely what it means to be a customer, to take on the burden of realisation and always necessarily be inadequate to it. Later, these students will be able to see themselves properly as obstacles to society, or perhaps, with lifelong learning, students will return having successfully diagnosed themselves as the problem.

Still, the dream of an undifferentiated labor that knows itself as superfluous is interrupted precisely by the labor of clearing away the burning roadblocks of ideology. While it is better that this police function be in the hands of the few, it still raises labor as difference, labor as the development of other labor, and therefore labor as a source of wealth. And although the enlightenment-type critique, as we suggest below, informs on, kisses the cheek of, any autonomous development as a result of this difference in labor, there is a break in the wall here, a shallow place in the river, a place to land under the rocks. The university still needs this clandestine labor to prepare this undifferentiated labor force, whose increasing specialisation and managerialist tendencies, again contra the restorationists, represent precisely the successful integration of the division of labor with the universe of exchange that commands restorationist loyalty.

Introducing this labor upon labor, and providing the space for its development, creates risks. Like the colonial police force recruited unwittingly from guerrilla neighborhoods, university labor may harbor refugees, fugitives, renegades, and castaways. But there are good reasons for the university to be confident that such elements will be exposed or forced underground. Precautions have been taken, book lists have been drawn up, teaching observations conducted, invitations to contribute made. Yet against these precautions stands the immanence of transcendence, the necessary deregulation and the possibilities of criminality and fugitivity that labor upon labor requires. Maroon communities of composition teachers, mentorless graduate students, adjunct Marxist historians, out or queer management professors, state college ethnic studies departments, closed-down film programs, visa-expired Yemeni student newspaper editors, historically black college sociologists, and feminist engineers. And what will the university say of them? It will say they are unprofessional. This is not an arbitrary charge. It is the charge against the more than professional. How do those who exceed the profession, who exceed and by exceeding escape, how do those maroons problematize themselves, problematize the university, force the university to consider them a problem, a danger? The undercommons is not, in short, the kind of fanciful communities of whimsy invoked by Bill Readings at the end of his book. The undercommons, its maroons, are always at war, always in hiding.

THERE IS NO DISTINCTION BETWEEN THE AMERICAN UNIVERSITY AND PROFESSIONALIZATION

But surely if one can write something on the surface of the university, if one can write for instance in the university about singularities – those events that refuse either the abstract or individual category of the bourgeois subject – one cannot say that there is no space in the university itself? Surely there is some space here for a theory, a conference, a book, a school of thought? Surely the university also makes thought possible? Is not the purpose of the university as Universitas, as liberal arts, to make the commons, make the public, make the nation of democratic citizenry? Is it not therefore important to protect this Universitas, whatever its impurities, from professionalization in the university? But we would ask what is already not possible in this talk in the hallways, among the buildings, in rooms of the university about possibility? How is the thought of the outside, as Gayatri Spivak means it, already not possible in this complaint?

The maroons know something about possibility. They are the condition of possibility of the production of knowledge in the university – the singularities against the writers of singularity, the writers who write, publish, travel, and speak. It is not merely a matter of the secret labor upon which such space is lifted, though of course such space is lifted from collective labor and by it. It is rather that to be a critical academic in the university is to be against the university, and to be against the university is always to recognize it and be recognized by it, and to institute the negligence of that internal outside, that unassimilated underground, a negligence of it that is precisely, we must insist, the basis of the professions. And this act of being against always already excludes the unrecognized modes of politics, the beyond of politics already in motion, the discredited criminal para-organization, what Robin Kelley might refer to as the infrapolitical field (and its music). It is not just the labor of the maroons but their prophetic organization that is negated by the idea of intellectual space in an organization called the university. This is why the negligence of the critical academic is always at the same time an assertion of bourgeois individualism.

Such negligence is the essence of professionalization where it turns out professionalization is not the opposite of negligence but its mode of politics in the United States. It takes the form of a choice that excludes the prophetic organization of the undercommons – to be against, to put into question the knowledge object, let us say in this case the university, not so much without touching its foundation, as without touching one's own condition of possibility, without admitting the Undercommons and being admitted to it. From this, a general negligence of condition is the only coherent position. Not so much an antifoundationalism or foundationalism, as both are used against each other to avoid contact with the undercommons. This always-negligent act is what leads us to say there is no distinction between the university in the United States and professionalization. There is no point in trying to hold out the university against its professionalization. They are the same. Yet the maroons refuse to refuse professionalization, that is, to be against the university. The university will not recognize this indecision, and thus professionalization is shaped precisely by what it cannot acknowledge, its internal antagonism, its wayward labor, its surplus. Against this wayward labor it sends the critical, sends its claim that what is left beyond the critical is waste.

But in fact, critical education only attempts to perfect professional education. The professions constitute themselves in an opposition to the unregulated and the ignorant without acknowledging the unregulated, ignorant, unprofessional labor that goes on not opposite them but within them. But if professional education ever slips in its labor, ever reveals its condition of possibility to the professions it supports and reconstitutes, critical education is there to pick it up, and to tell it, never mind – it was just a bad dream, the ravings, the drawings of the mad. Because critical education is precisely there to tell professional education to rethink its relationship to its opposite – by which critical education means both itself and the unregulated, against which professional education is deployed. In other words, critical education arrives to support any faltering negligence, to be vigilant in its negligence, to be critically engaged in its negligence. It is more than an ally of professional education, it is its attempted completion.

A professional education has become a critical education. But one should not applaud this fact. It should be taken for what it is, not progress in the professional schools, not cohabitation with the Universitas, but counterinsurgency, the refounding terrorism of law, coming for the discredited, coming for those who refuse to write off or write up the undercommons.

The Universitas is always a state/State strategy. Perhaps it's surprising to say professionalization – that which reproduces the professions – is a state strategy. Certainly, critical academic professionals tend to be regarded today as harmless intellectuals, malleable, perhaps capable of some modest intervention in the so-called public sphere. But to see how this underestimates the presence of the state we can turn to a bad reading of Derrida's consideration of Hegel's 1822 report to the Prussian Minister of Education. Derrida notices the way that Hegel rivals the state in his ambition for education, wanting to put into place a progressive pedagogy of philosophy designed to support Hegel's worldview, to unfold as encyclopedic. This ambition both mirrors the state's ambition, because it, too, wants to control education and to impose a worldview, and threatens it, because Hegel's State exceeds and thus localises the Prussian state, exposing its pretense to the encyclopedic. Derrida draws the following lesson from his reading: the Universitas, as he generalizes the university (but specifies it, too, as properly intellectual and not professional), always has the impulse of State, or enlightenment, and the impulse of state, or its specific conditions of production and reproduction. Both have the ambition to be, as Derrida says, onto- and auto-encyclopedic. It follows that to be either for the Universitas or against it presents problems. To be for the Universitas is to support this onto- and auto-encyclopedic project of the State as enlightenment, or enlightenment as totality, to use an old-fashioned word. To be too much against the Universitas, however, creates the danger of specific elements in the state taking steps to rid itself of the contradiction of the onto- and auto-encyclopedic project of the Universitas and replacing it with some other form of social reproduction, the anti-enlightenment – the position, for instance, of New Labour in Britain and of the states of New York and California with their "teaching institutions." But a bad reading of Derrida will also yield our question again: what is lost in this undecidability? What is the price of refusing to be either for the Universitas or for professionalization, to be critical of both, and who pays that price? Who makes it possible to reach the aporia of this reading? Who works in the premature excess of totality, in the not not-ready of negligence?

The mode of professionalization that is the American university is precisely dedicated to promoting this consensual choice: an antifoundational critique of the University or a foundational critique of the university. Taken as choices, or hedged as bets, one tempered with the other, they are nonetheless always negligent. Professionalization is built on this choice. It rolls out into ethics and efficiency, responsibility and science, and numerous other choices, all built upon the theft, the conquest, the negligence of the outcast mass intellectuality of the undercommons.

It is therefore unwise to think of professionalization as a narrowing and better to think of it as a circling, an encircling of war wagons around the last camp of indigenous women and children. Think about the way the American doctor or lawyer regard themselves as educated, enclosed in the circle of the state's encyclopedia, though they may know nothing of philosophy or history. What would be outside this act of the conquest circle, what kind of ghostly labored world escapes in the circling act, an act like a kind of broken phenomenology where the brackets never come back off and what is experienced as knowledge is the absolute horizon of knowledge whose name is banned by the banishment of the absolute. It is simply a horizon that does not bother to make itself possible. No wonder that whatever their origins or possibilities, it is theories of pragmatism in the United States and critical realism in Britain that command the loyalty of critical intellectuals. Never having to confront the foundation, never having to confront antifoundation out of faith in the unconfrontable foundation, critical intellectuals can float in the middle range. These loyalties banish dialectics with its inconvenient interest in pushing the material and abstract, the table and its brain, as far as it can, unprofessional behavior at its most obvious.

PROFESSIONALIZATION IS THE PRIVATIZATION OF THE SOCIAL INDIVIDUAL THROUGH NEGLIGENCE

centrality
negligent of
critical to
education

Surely professionalization brings with it the benefits of competence. It may be the onto- and auto-encyclopedic circle of the university particular to the American state, but is it not possible to recuperate something from this knowledge for practical advances? Or, indeed, is it not possible to embark on critical projects within its terrain, projects that would turn its competencies to more radical ends? No, we would say, it is not. And saying so we prepare to part company with American critical academics, to become unreliable, to be disloyal to the public sphere, to be obstructive and shiftless, dumb with insolence in the face of the call to critical thinking.

Let us, as an example, act disloyally to the field of public administration and especially in masters of public administration programs, including related programs in public health, environmental management, nonprofit and arts management, and the large menu of human services courses, certificates, diplomas, and degrees that underpin this disciplinary cluster. It is difficult not to sense that these programs exist against themselves, that they despise themselves. (Although later one can see that as with all professionalization, it is the underlying negligence that unsettles the surface of labor power.) The average lecture, in the Robert F. Wagner Graduate School of Public Service at NYU for instance, may be more antistatist, more skeptical of government, more modest in its social policy goals than the average lecture in the avowedly neoclassical economics or new right political science departments at that same university. It would not be much different at Syracuse University, or a dozen other prominent public administration schools. One might say that skepticism is an important part of higher education, but this particular skepticism is not founded on close study of the object in question. In fact, there is no state theory in public administration programs in the United States. Instead, the state is regarded as the proverbial devil we know. And whether it is understood in public administration as a necessary evil, or as a good that is nonetheless of limited usefulness and availability, it is always entirely knowable as an object. Therefore it is not so much that these programs are set against themselves. It is rather that they are set against some students, and particularly those who come to public administration with a sense of what Derrida has called a duty beyond duty, or a passion.

To be skeptical of what one already knows is of course an absurd position. If one is skeptical of an object then one is already in the position of not knowing that object, and if one claims to know the object, one cannot also claim to be skeptical of that object, which amounts to being skeptical of one's own claim. But this is the position of professionalization, and it is this position that confronts that student, however rare, who comes to public administration with a passion. Any attempt at passion, at stepping out of this skepticism of the known into an inadequate confrontation with what exceeds it and oneself, must be suppressed by this professionalization. This is not merely a matter of administering the world, but of administering away the world (and with it prophecy). Any other disposition is not only unprofessional but incompetent, unethical, and irresponsible, bordering on the criminal. Again the discipline of public administration is particularly, though not uniquely, instructive, both in its pedagogy and in its scholarship, and offers the chance to be disloyal, to smash and grab what it locks up.

Public administration holds to the idea both in the lecture hall and the professional journal that its categories are knowable. The state, the economy, and civil society may change size or shape, labor may enter or exit, and ethical consideration may vary, but these objects are both positivistic and normative, standing in discrete, spatial arrangement each to the other. Professionalization begins by accepting these categories precisely so competence can be invoked, a competence that at the same time guards its own foundation (like Michael Dukakis riding around in a tank phantasmatically patrolling his empty neighborhood). This responsibility for the preservation of objects becomes precisely that Weberian site-specific ethics that has the effect, as Theodor Adorno recognized, of naturalizing the production of capitalist sites. To question them thus becomes not only incompetent and unethical but the enactment of a security breach.

For instance, if one wanted to explore the possibility that public administration might best be defined as the labor of the relentless privatization of capitalist society, one could gain a number of unprofessional insights. It would help explain the inadequacy of the three major strains in public administration scholarship in the United States. The public ethos strain represented by projects like refounding public administration, and the journal *Administration and Society*; the public competence strain represented in the debate between public administration and the new public management, and the journal Public Administration Review; and the critical strain represented by PAT-Net, the Public Administration Theory Network, and its journal *Administrative Theory & Praxis*. If public administration is the competence to confront the socialisation thrown up continuously by capitalism and to take as much of that socialisation as possible and reduce it either to something called the public or something called the private, then immediately all three scholarly positions become invalid. It is not possible to speak of a labor that is dedicated to the reproduction of social dispossession as having an ethical dimension. It is not possible to decide the efficiency or scope of such labor after the fact of its expenditure in this operation by looking at it once it has reproduced something called the public or something called the private. And it is not possible to be critical and at the same time to accept uncritically the foundation of public administrationist thought in these spheres of the public and private, and to deny the labor that goes on behind the backs of these categories, in the undercommons, of, for instance, the republic of women who run Brooklyn.

But this is an unprofessional example. It does preserve the rules and respect the terms of the debate, enter the speech community, by knowing and dwelling in its (unapproachable) foundational objects. It is also an incompetent example. It does not allow itself to be measured, applied, and improved, except to be found wanting. And it is an unethical example. Suggesting the utter dominance of one category over another – is this not fascism or communism? Finally, it is a passionate example full of prophecy not proof, a bad example of a weak argument making no attempt to defend itself, given over to some kind of sacrifice of the professional community emanating from the undercommons. Such is the negligent opinion of professional public administration scholars.

What, further, is the connection then between this professionalization as the onto- and auto-encyclopedia of the American state and the spread of professionalization beyond the university or perhaps the spread of the university beyond the university, and with the colonies of the undercommons? A certain riot into which professionalization stumbles – when the care of the social is confronted with its reaction, enforced negligence – a riot erupts and the professional looks absurd, like a recruiting booth at a carnival, professional services, personal professional services, turning pro to pay for university. It is at this riotous moment that professionalization shows its desperate business, nothing less than to convert the social individual. Except perhaps, something more, the ultimate goal of counterinsurgency everywhere: to turn the insurgents into state agents.

CRITICAL ACADEMICS ARE THE PROFESSIONALS PAR EXCELLENCE

The critical academic questions the university, questions the state, questions art, politics, culture. But in the undercommons it is "no questions asked." It is unconditional – the door swings open for refuge even though it may let in police agents and destruction. The questions are superfluous in the undercommons. If you don't know, why ask? The only question left on the surface is what can it mean to be critical when the professional defines himself or herself as one who is critical of negligence, while negligence defines professionalization? Would it not mean that to be critical of the university would make one the professional *par excellence*, more negligent than any other? To distance oneself professionally through critique, is this not the most active consent to privatize the social individual? The undercommons might by contrast be understood as wary of critique, weary of it, and at the same time dedicated to the collectivity of its future, the collectivity that may come to be its future. The undercommons in some ways tries to escape from critique and its degradation as university-consciousness and self-consciousness about university-consciousness, retreating, as Adrian Piper says, into the external world.

This maroon community, if it exists, therefore also seeks to escape the fiat of the ends of man. The sovereign's army of academic antihumanism will pursue this negative community into the undercommons, seeking to conscript it, needing to conscript it. But as seductive as this critique may be, as provoked as it may be, in the undercommons they know it is not love. Between the fiat of the ends and the ethics of new beginnings, the undercommons abides, and some find comfort in this. Comfort for the emigrants from conscription, not to be ready for humanity and who must endure the return of humanity nonetheless, as it may be endured by those who will or must endure it, as certainly those of the undercommons endure it, always in the break, always the supplement of the *general intellect* and its source. When the critical academic who lives by fiat (of others) gets no answer, no commitment, from the undercommons, well then certainly the conclusion will come: they are not practical, not serious about change, not rigorous, not productive.

Meanwhile, that critical academic in the university, in the circle of the American state, questions the university. He claims to be critical of the negligence of the university. But is he not the most accomplished professional in his studied negligence? If the labor upon labor, the labor among labor of the unprofessionals in the university sparks revolt, retreat, release, does the labor of the critical academic not involve a mockery of this first labor, a performance that is finally in its lack of concern for what it parodies, negligent? Does the questioning of the critical academic not become a pacification? Or, to put it plainly, does the critical academic not teach how to deny precisely what one produces with others, and is this not the lesson the professions return to the university to learn again and again? Is the critical academic then not dedicated to what Michael E. Brown termed the impoverishment, the immiseration, of society's cooperative prospects? This is the professional course of action. This enlightenment-type charade is utterly negligent in its critique, a negligence that disavows the possibility of a thought of an outside, a nonplace called the undercommons – the nonplace that must be thought outside to be sensed inside, from which the enlightenment-type charade has stolen everything for its game.

But if the critical academic is merely a professional, why spend so much time on him? Why not just steal his books one morning and give them to deregistered students in a closed-down and beery student bar, where the seminar on burrowing and borrowing takes place. Yet we must speak of these critical academics because negligence it turns out is a major crime of state.

INCARCERATION IS THE PRIVATIZATION OF THE SOCIAL INDIVIDUAL THROUGH WAR

If one were to insist, the opposite of professionalization is that fugitive impulse to rely on the undercommons for protection, to rely on the honor, and to insist on the honor of the fugitive community; if one were to insist, the opposite of professionalization is that criminal impulse to steal from professions, from the university, with neither apologies nor malice, to steal the enlightenment for others, to steal oneself with a certain blue music, a certain tragic optimism, to steal away with mass intellectuality; if one were to do this, would this not be to place criminality and negligence against each other? Would it not place professionalization, would it not place the university, against honor? And what then could be said for criminality?

Perhaps then it needs to be said that the crack dealer, terrorist, and political prisoner share a commitment to war, and society responds in kind with wars on crime, terror, drugs, communism. But "this war on the commitment to war" crusades as a war against the asocial, that is, those who live "without a concern for sociality." Yet it cannot be such a thing. After all, it is professionalization itself that is devoted to the asocial, the university itself that reproduces the knowledge of how to neglect sociality in its very concern for what it calls asociality. No, this war against the commitment to war responds to this commitment to war as the threat that it is – not mere negligence or careless destruction but a commitment against the idea of society itself, that is, against what Foucault called *the conquest*, the unspoken war that founded, and with the force of law, refounds society. Not asocial but against the social, this is the commitment to war, and this is what disturbs and at the same time forms the undercommons against the university.

Is this not the way to understand incarceration in the United States today? And understanding it, can we not say that it is precisely the fear that the criminal will rise to challenge the negligence that leads to the need, in the context of the American state and its particularly violent Universitas circle, to concentrate always on conquest denial?

THE UNIVERSITY IS THE SITE OF THE SOCIAL REPRODUCTION OF CONQUEST DENIAL

Here one comes face to face with the roots of professional and critical commitment to negligence, to the depths of the impulse to deny the thought of the internal outside among critical intellectuals, and the necessity for professionals to question without question. Whatever else they do, critical intellectuals who have found space in the university are always already performing the denial of the new society when they deny the undercommons, when they find that space on the surface of the university, and when they join the conquest denial by improving that space. Before they criticise the aesthetic and the Aesthetic, the state and the State, history and History, they have already practiced the operation of denying what makes these categories possible in the underlabor of their social being as critical academics.

The slogan on the Left, then, "universities, not jails," marks a choice that may not be possible. In other words, perhaps more universities promote more jails. Perhaps it is necessary finally to see that the university produces incarceration as the product of its negligence. Perhaps there is another relation between the University and the Prison – beyond simple opposition or family resemblance – that the undercommons reserves as the object and inhabitation of another abolitionism. What might appear as the professionalization of the American university, our starting point, now might better be understood as a certain intensification of method in the Universitas, a tightening of the circle. Professionalization cannot take over the American university – it is the critical approach of the university, its Universitas. And indeed, it appears now that this state with its peculiar violent hegemony must deny what Foucault called in his 1975-76 lectures the race war.

War on the commitment to war breaks open the memory of the conquest. The new American studies should do this, too, if it is to be not just a people's history of the same country but a movement against the possibility of a country, or any other; not just property justly distributed on the border but property unknown. And there are other spaces situated between the Universitas and the undercommons, spaces that are characterized precisely by not having space. Thus the fire aimed at black studies by everyone from William Bennett to Henry Louis Gates Jr., and the proliferation of Centers without affiliation to the memory of the conquest, to its living guardianship, to the protection of its honor, to the nights of labor, in the undercommons.

The university, then, is not the opposite of the prison, since they are both involved in their way with the reduction and command of the social individual. And indeed, under the circumstances, more universities and fewer prisons would, it has to be concluded, mean the memory of the war was being further lost, and living unconquered, conquered labor abandoned to its lowdown fate. Instead, the undercommons takes the prison as a secret about the conquest, but a secret, as Sara Ahmed says, whose growing secrecy is its power, its ability to keep a distance between it and its revelation, a secret that calls into being the prophetic, a secret held in common, organized as secret, calling into being the prophetic organization.

THE UNDERCOMMONS OF THE UNIVERSITY IS A NONPLACE OF ABOLITION

Ruth Wilson Gilmore: "Racism is the state-sanctioned and/or extra-legal production and exploitation of group differentiated vulnerabilities to premature (social, civil and/or corporeal) death." What is the difference between this and slavery? What is, so to speak, the object of abolition? Not so much the abolition of prisons but the abolition of a society that could have prisons, that could have slavery, that could have the wage, and therefore not abolition as the elimination of anything but abolition as the founding of a new society. The object of abolition then would have a resemblance to communism that would be, to return to Spivak, uncanny. The uncanny that disturbs the critical going on above it, the professional going on without it, the uncanny that one can sense in prophecy, the strangely known moment, the gathering content, of a cadence, and the uncanny that one can sense in cooperation, the secret once called solidarity. The uncanny feeling we are left with is that something else is there in the under-commons. It is the prophetic organization that works for the red and black abolition!

BLACKNESS AND

GOVERNANCE

1. There is an anoriginary drive whose fateful internal difference (as opposed to fatal flaw) is that it brings regulation into existence, into a history irregularly punctuated by transformations that drive imposes upon regulation. Those transformative impositions show up for us now as compensation and surplus: as the payment of a massive and incalculable debt by the ones who not only never promised it; and as the massive and incalculable range of labored living, "the thing realized in things…the universality of individual needs, capacities, pleasures, productive forces, etc., created through universal exchange" that Marx called wealth. The anoriginary drive and the insistences it calls into being and moves through, that criminality that brings the law online, the runaway anarchic ground of unpayable debt and untold wealth, the fugal, internal world theater that shows up for a minute serially – poor but extravagant as opposed to frugal – is blackness which must be understood in its ontological difference from black people who are, nevertheless, (under)privileged insofar as they are given (to) an understanding of it.

2. Consider the following statement: "There's nothing wrong with blackness": What if this were the primitive axiom of a new black studies underived from the psycho-politico-pathology of populations and its corollary theorisation of the state or of state racism; an axiom

derived, as all such axioms are, from the "runaway tongues" and elo-
quent vulgarities encrypted in works and days that turn out to be of
the native or the slave only insofar as the fugitive is misrecognized,
and in bare lives that turn out to be bare only insofar as no attention
is paid to them, only insofar as such lives persist under the sign and
weight of a closed question?

3. The black aesthetic turns on a dialectic of luxuriant withholding – abundance and lack push technique over the edge of refusal so
that the trouble with beauty, which is the very animation and emana-
tion of art, is always and everywhere troubled again and again. New
technique, new beauty. At the same time, the black aesthetic is not
about technique, is not a technique, though a fundamental element
of the terror-driven anaesthetic disavowal of "our terribleness" is the
eclectic sampling of techniques of black performativity in the interest
of the unproblematically dispossessive assertion of an internal difference, complexity or syntax which was always and everywhere so apparent that the assertion is a kind of self-indulgent, self-exculpatory
superfluity. Such assertion amounts to an attempt to refute claims
of blackness's atomic simplicity that have never been serious enough
to refute (as they were made unfalsifiably, without evidence, by way
of unreasonable though wholly rationalized motivations, in bad faith
and dogmatic slumber).

4. The dismissal of any possible claim regarding the essence or
even the being of blackness (*in its irreducible performativity*) becomes,
itself, the dismissal of blackness. Differential or differentiating techniques are made to account and stand in for an absence. Appeals to
internal difference are made in order to disallow instantiation. Abstraction of or from the referent is seen as tantamount to its non-
existence. The techniques of black performance – in their manifest
difference from one another, in the full range of their transferability
and in their placement within a history that is structured but not

determined by imposition – are understood to constitute the "proof" that blackness is not or is lost or is loss. In this regard, abstraction and performativity are meant to carry some of the same weight where the refutation of claims about the authenticity or unity of blackness becomes the refutation of blackness as such. This appeal to technique is, itself, a technique of governance. Meanwhile blackness means to render unanswerable the question of how to govern the thing that loses and finds itself to be what it is not.

5. Not in the interest either of some simple or complex opposition of *Technik* and *Eigentlichkeit*, but rather in the improvisation through their opposition moves the black aesthetic. What is the content of (your) (black) technique? What is the essence of (your) (black) performance? An imperative is implied here: to pay attention to (black) performances since it is left to those who pay such attention to re-theorize essence, representation, abstraction, performance, being.

6. Disavowal is a tendency inherent in the black radical tradition, a kind of inevitability that emerges from the pathologically auto-critical force of a more genuine (anticipatory variant of) enlightenment, on the one hand, and the more basic – which is not but nothing other than to say base – desires that animate the *ideology of uplift*. The logic of correction is political instrumentality's fugitive, though such fugitivity has a doubled, self-consumptive edge – the pathological drive of the pathologist; the end of an anti-essentialist anti-racism without the necessary re-routing. Such instrumentality can very quickly turn sour or get turned out in the interest of empire (artists against art in the interest of gold, prefabricated knockoffs – with readymade provenances – of a certain New York intellectuality, a state of mind, a state mind, a mind of the United States of Exception, of the unoriginal gangsters of The American Century who stole modern art from the ones who stole away as modern art, the moving, motley, sculptural, animated, theatrical things).

7. But blackness still has work to do: to discover the re-routing encoded in the work of art: in the anachoreographic reset of a shoulder, in the quiet extremities that animate a range of social chromaticisms and, especially, in the mutations that drive mute, labored, musicked speech as it moves between an incapacity for reasoned or meaningful self-generated utterance that is, on the one hand, supposed and, on the other hand, imposed, and a critical predisposition to steal (away). In those mutations that are always also a regendering or transgendering (as in Al Green's errant falsetto or Big Maybelle's bass – which is not but nothing other than basic – growl), and in between that impropriety of speech that approaches animality and a tendency towards expropriation that approaches criminality, lies blackness, lies the black thing that cuts the regulative, governant force of (the) understanding (and even of those understandings of blackness to which black people are given since fugitivity escapes even the fugitive).

8. The work of blackness is inseparable from the violence of blackness. Violence is where technique and beauty come back, though they had never left. Consider technique as a kind of strain and consider the technique that is embedded in and cuts techniques – the (Fanonian as apposed to Artaudian) cruelty. The internal difference of blackness is a violent and cruel re-routing, by way and outside of critique, that is predicated on the notion, which was given to me, at least, by Martin Luther Kilson, Jr., that there's *nothing wrong with us* (precisely insofar as there is something wrong, something off, something ungovernably, fugitively living in us that is constantly taken for the pathogen it instantiates). This notion is manifest primarily in the long, slow motion – the series of tragically pleasurable detours – of the immediate (of improvisation, which is something not but almost nothing other than the spontaneous), a re-routing that turns away from a turning on or to itself. The apposition of Fanonian and Artaudian cruelty is an itinerancy that bridges life and blackness. Movement towards and against death and its specific and general prematurities and a willingness to break the law one calls into existence constitute their very

relationality. But what's the relation between willingness and propensity? And what's the difference between flight and fatality? What are the politics of being ready to die and what have they to do with the scandal of enjoyment? What is premature death? What commerce ensues between what Jacques Lacan identifies as man's specific prematurity of birth and what Hussein Abdilahi Bulhan identifies as the specific (and irreducible threat of) prematurity of death in blackness?

9. Addressing these questions demands some attempt to discover how blackness operates as the modality of life's constant escape and takes the form, the held and errant pattern, of flight. So we've been trying to find out how the commons cuts common sense – the necessarily failed administrative accounting of the incalculable – that is the object/ive of enlightenment self-control; and trying to get with that undercommon sensuality, that radical occupied-elsewhere, that utopic commonunderground of this dystopia, the funked-up here and now of this anacentric particularity that we occupy and with which we are preoccupied. It must be that in exploring the black market underside of this constant economy of misrecognition, this misery cognition, it will be possible to discover the informal, form-giving pleasures of the content economy: because we're in love with the way the beat of this slum-like deictic circle flies off the handle; how event music, full of color, blows up the event horizon; how the soundwaves from this black hole carry flavorful pictures to touch; how the only way to get with them is to sense them. This information can never be lost, only irrevocably given in transit. We could never provide a whole bunch of smooth transitions for this order of ditches and hidden spans. There's just this open seriality of terminals in off transcription. Some people want to run things, other things want to run. If they ask you, tell them we were flying. Knowledge of freedom is (in) the invention of escape, stealing away in the confines, in the form, of a break. This is held close in the open song of the ones who are supposed to be silent.

10.

Whom do we mean when we say "there's nothing wrong with us"? The fat ones. The ones who are out of all compass however precisely they are located. The ones who are not conscious when they listen to Les McCann. The Screamers who don't say much, insolently. The churchgoers who value impropriety. The ones who manage to evade self-management in the enclosure. The ones without interest who bring the muted noise and mutant grammar of the new general interest by refusing. The new general intellect extending the long, extra-genetic line of extra-moral obligation to disturb and evade intelligence. Our cousins. All our friends.

11.

The new general intellect is rich. And the new regulation wants to give you back what you got, publicly, which is to say partly, what can only be owed. This regulation is called governance. It is not governmentality nor is it a governance of the soul. It must be described in its inscription in that criminality that doubles as debt, that doubles the debt, that twists in inscription, that torques.

Nikolas Rose had it wrong, governance is not about government, and Foucault might have got it right. But how could he know if he could not find the priority of what he knew in North Africa? Governance is the wit of the colonial official, the CIA woman, the NGO man. Will we be in on the joke now that we all know governmentality so well? We can all read it like a book. Nothing goes on behind the backs of the new cynicism (except we need to remind Paolo Virno of what always went on beyond cynicism, what was always without home and shelter, was always outnumbered and outgunned). Will we be in on the joke of religion, of white trash, or the joke of development, of Marxism? When Gayatri Spivak refuses to laugh, she is told she wants to deny the workers their cappuccini. She holds out for reduction against the insider trading of domination, she holds out for a reduction against the coercion that exploits what it cannot reduce to an invitation to governance.

Still the invitations arrive through the smirk of governmentality by all, or on the severe and serious brow of democratisation. Critique and policy. No wonder Rose thought governance was about government. Worse still some say that governance is merely a management neologism, a piece of old-fashioned ideology. Others think governance is simply a retreat to liberalism from the market fundamentalism of neoliberalism.

But we want to reduce it up to a kind of 'state-thought,' a form of thought which for Gilles Deleuze and Felix Guattari supported the rendering and hording of social wealth. A thought that thinks away the private before the public and the private, but not exactly before, rather a step ahead. State-thought says "they burnt down their own neighbourhood." Not theirs, before theirs. But then nobody writes about the state any more, because governance is too clever for that, governance invites us to laugh at the state, to look back at it, its political immaturity in the face of governmentality by all, its dangerous behaviour, its laziness, its blackness. Which means really the exhaustion of blackness thought by the state and the new way to steal from the stolen, who refuse to give up the secret of thieving with their theft, the secret of their thieving of their theft.

In the newest language of the social sciences we might say that governance is generated by a refusal among biopolitical populations. Or perhaps by the self-activity of immaterial labor. But maybe we would like to say it is provoked by the *communicability of unmanageable racial and sexual difference,* insisting on a now unfathomable debt of wealth.

12. Governance is a strategy for the privatization of social reproductive labor, a strategy provoked by this communicability, infected by it, hosting and hostile. As Toni Negri says "the new face of productive labor (intellectual, relational, linguistic, and affective, rather than physical, individual, muscular, instrumental) does not understate but accentuates the corporality and materiality of labor." But accumulating collective cognitive and affective labor from these highly communicable

differences is not the same as accumulating biopolitical bodies that labor. Differences here matter not for order, but order matters for differences. The order that collects differences, the order that collects what Marx called labor still objectifying itself, is the order of governance.

13. But governance collects like a drill boring for samples. Governance is a form of prospecting for this immaterial labor. Immaterial labor is opaque to state-thought until it becomes labor-power, exchangeable potentiality. Immaterial labor could easily be mistaken for life, which is why the biopolitical must take a new form. A form that provokes life to give up this new potential. Corporate social responsibility is sincere. The invitation to governmentality is made by way of transfer of responsibility, and immaterial labor is distinguished from the vitality of life, from its vessel, by the taking up of responsibility, and life is now distinguished by its overt irresponsibility.

Since neither the state nor capital know where to find immaterial labor or how to distinguish it from life, governance is a kind of exploratory drilling with a responsibility bit. But this drilling is not really for labor-power. It is for politics, or rather as Tiziana Terranova suggests, it is for soft control, the cultivation of politics below the political. The slogan of governance might be not 'where there is gas, there is oil,' but 'where there is politics there is labor,' a kind of labor that might be provoked, in the words of critique, or grown, in the words of policy, into labor-power. But this labor as subjectivity is not politics to itself. It must be politicised if it is to yield up its labor-power, or rather we might say, politics is the refining process for immaterial labor. Politicisation is the work of state-thought, the work today, of capital. This is the interest it bears. And interests are its lifeblood, its labor.

14. Governance operates through the apparent auto-generation of these interests. Unlike previous regimes of sovereignty, there is no predetermined interest (no nation, no constitution, no language)

to be realized collectively. Rather interests are solicited, offered up, and accumulated. But this is a moment so close to life, to vitality, to the body, so close to no interests, that the imposition of self-management becomes imperative. That imposition is governance.

15. Governance then becomes the management of self-management. The generation of interests appears as wealth, plentitude, potential. It hides the waste of the raw immaterial and its reproduction in the hurry of its conferences, consultations, and outreach. Indeed within the firm, self-management is distinguished from obedience by the generation of new interests in quality, design, discipline, and communication. But with the implosion of the time and space in the firm, with the dispersion and virtualisation of productivity, governance arrives to manage self-management, not from above, but from below. What comes up then may not be value from below as Toni Negri calls it, but politics from below, such that we have to be wary of the grassroots and suspicious of the community. When what emerges from below is interests, when value from below becomes politics from below, self-management has been realized, and governance has done its work.

16. The Soviets used to say that the United States had free speech but no one could hear you over the noise of the machines. Today no one can hear you over the noise of talk. Maurizio Lazzarato says immaterial labor is loquacious and industrial labor was mute. Governance populations are gregarious. Gregariousness is the exchange form of immaterial labor-power, a labor-power summoned by interests from a communicability without interest, a viral communicability, a beat.

The compulsion to tell us how you feel is the compulsion of labor, not citizenship, exploitation not domination, and it is whiteness. Whiteness is why Lazzarato does not hear industrial labor. Whiteness is nothing but a relationship to blackness as we have tried to describe it here, but in particular a relationship to blackness in its relationship to capital, which is to say the movement from muteness to dumb insolence which may be by way of bringing the noise. But the noise of talk, white noise, the information-rich environment of the gregarious, comes from subjectivities formed of objectified labor. These are the subjectivities of interests, subjectivities of labor-power whose potentialities are already bounded by how they will be spent, and mute to their blackness. This is the real muteness of industrial labor. And it is the real gregariousness of immaterial labor. Governance is the extension of whiteness on a global scale.

17. NGOs are the laboratories of governance. The premise of the NGO is that all populations must become gregarious. And the ethics of the NGOs, the dream of governance in general, is to go beyond representation as a form of sovereignty, to auto-generating representation, in the double sense. Those who can represent themselves will also be those who re-present themselves as interests in one and the same move, collapsing the distinction. The NGO is the research and development arm of governance finding new ways to bring to blackness what it is said to lack, the thing that cannot be brought, interests. I don't want to speak for those people is the mantra of governance.

18. Governance is the putting to work of democracy. When representation becomes the obligation of all, when politics becomes the work of all, democracy is labored. No longer can democracy promise the return of something lost in the workplace, but rather becomes itself an extension of the workplace. And even democracy cannot contain governance, but is only a tool in its box. Governance is always generated, always organic to any situation. Democracy sits badly in many situations, and must be worked at, made to appear as natural as governance, made to serve governance.

19. Because governance is the annunciation of universal exchange. The exchange through communication of all institutional forms, all forms of exchange value with each other is the enunciation of governance. The hospital talks to the prison which talks to the university which talks to the NGO which talks to the corporation through governance, and not just to each other but about each other. Everybody knows everything about our biopolitics. This is the perfection of democracy under the general equivalent. It is also the annunciation of governance as the realisation of universal exchange on the grounds of capitalism.

20. Governance and criminality – the condition of being without interests – come to make each other possible. What would it mean to struggle against governance, against that which can produce struggle by germinating interests? When governance is understood as the criminalisation of being without interests, as a regulation brought into being by criminality, where criminality is that excess left from criminalisation, a certain fragility emerges, a certain limit, an uncertain imposition by a greater drive, the mere utterance of whose name has again become too black, too strong altogether.

DEBT AND STUDY

credit – privatisation
debt – socialization

DEBT AND CREDIT

They say we have too much debt. We need better credit, more credit, less spending. They offer us credit repair, credit counseling, microcredit, personal financial planning. They promise to match credit and debt again, debt and credit. But our debts stay bad. We keep buying another song, another round. It is not credit we seek nor even debt but bad debt which is to say real debt, the debt that cannot be repaid, the debt at a distance, the debt without creditor, the black debt, the queer debt, the criminal debt. Excessive debt, incalculable debt, debt for no reason, debt broken from credit, debt as its own principle.

Credit is a means of privatization and debt a means of socialisation. So long as they pair in the monogamous violence of the home, the pension, the government, or the university, debt can only feed credit, debt can only desire credit. And credit can only expand by means of debt. But debt is social and credit is asocial. Debt is mutual. Credit runs only one way. But debt runs in every direction, scatters, escapes, seeks refuge. The debtor seeks refuge among other debtors, acquires debt from them, offers debt to them. The place of refuge is the place to which you can only owe more and more because there is no creditor, no payment possible. This refuge, this place of bad debt, is what we call the fugitive public. Running through the public and the private, the state and the economy, the fugitive public cannot be known by its bad debt but only by bad debtors. To creditors it is just a place where something is wrong, though that something wrong – the invaluable thing, the thing that has no value – is desired. Creditors seek to demolish that place, that project, in order to save the ones who live there from themselves and their lives.

They research it, gather information on it, try to calculate it. They want to save it. They want to break its concentration and put the fragments in the bank. But all of a sudden, the thing credit cannot know, the fugitive thing for which it gets no credit, is inescapable.

Once you start to see bad debt, you start to see it everywhere, hear it everywhere, feel it everywhere. This is the real crisis for credit, its real crisis of accumulation. Now debt begins to accumulate without it. That's what makes it so bad. We saw it in a step yesterday, some hips, a smile, the way a hand moved. We heard it in a break, a cut, a lilt, the way the words leapt. We felt it in the way someone saves the best stuff just to give it to you and then its gone, given, a debt. They don't want nothing. You have got to accept it, you have got to accept that. You're in debt but you can't give credit because they won't hold it. Then the phone rings. It's the creditors. Credit keeps track. Debt forgets. You're not home, you're not you, you moved without a forwarding address called refuge.

The student is not home, out of time, out of place, without credit, in bad debt. The student is a bad debtor threatened with credit. The student runs from credit. Credit pursues the student, offering to match credit for debt, until enough debts and enough credits have piled up. But the student has a habit, a bad habit. She studies. She studies but she does not learn. If she learned they could measure her progress, establish her attributes, give her credit. But the student keeps studying, keeps planning to study, keeps running to study, keeps studying a plan, keeps elaborating a debt. The student does not intend to pay.

DEBT AND FORGETTING

Debt cannot be forgiven, it can only be forgotten to be remembered again. To forgive debt is to restore credit. It is restorative justice. Debt can be abandoned for bad debt. It can be forgotten for bad debt, but it cannot be forgiven. Only creditors can forgive, and only debtors, bad debtors, can offer justice. Creditors forgive debt to offer credit, to offer the very source of the pain of debt, a pain for which there is only one justice, bad debt, forgetting, remembering again, remembering it cannot be paid, cannot be credited, stamped received. There will be a jubilee when the North spends its own money, is left with nothing, and spends again, on credit, on stolen cards, on a friend who knows he will never see that again. There will be a jubilee when the Global South does not get credit for discounted contributions to world civilisation and commerce but keeps its debts, changes them only for the debts of others, a swap among those who never intend to pay, who will never be allowed to pay, in a bar in Penang, in Port of Spain, in Bandung, where your credit is no good.

Credit can be restored, restructured, rehabilitated, but debt forgiven is always unjust, always unforgiven. Restored credit is restored justice and restorative justice is always the renewed reign of credit, a reign of terror, a hail of obligations to be met, measured, meted, endured. Justice is only possible where debt never obliges, never demands, never equals credit, payment, payback. Justice is possible only where it is never asked, in the refuge of bad debt, in the fugitive public of strangers not communities, of undercommons not neighbourhoods, among those who have been there all along from somewhere. To seek justice through restoration is to return debt to the balance sheet and the balance sheet never balances. It plunges toward risk, volatility, uncertainty, more credit chasing more debt, more debt shackled to credit. To restore is not to conserve, again. There is no refuge in restoration. Conservation is always new. It comes from the place we stopped while we were on the run. It's made from the people who took us in. It's the space they say is wrong, the practice they say needs fixing, the homeless aneconomics of visiting.

Fugitive publics do not need to be restored. They need to be conserved, which is to say moved, hidden, restarted with the same joke, the same story, always elsewhere than where the long arm of the creditor seeks them, conserved from restoration, beyond justice, beyond law, in bad country, in bad debt. They are planned when they are least expected, planned when they don't follow the process, planned when they escape policy, evade governance, forget themselves, remember themselves, have no need of being forgiven. They are not wrong though they are not, finally communities; they are debtors at distance, bad debtors, forgotten but never forgiven. Give credit where credit is due, and render unto bad debtors only debt, only that mutuality that tells you what you can't do. You can't pay me back, give me credit, get free of me, and I can't let you go when you're gone. If you want to do something, forget this debt, and remember it later.

Debt at a distance is forgotten, and remembered again. Think of autonomism, its debt at a distance to the black radical tradition. In autonomia, in the militancy of post-workerism, there is no outside, refusal takes place inside and makes its break, its flight, its exodus from the inside. There is biopolitical production and there is empire. There is even what Franco 'Bifo' Berardi calls soul trouble. In other words there is this debt at a distance to a global politics of blackness emerging out of slavery and colonialism, a black radical politics, a politics of debt without payment, without credit, without limit. This debt was built in a struggle with empire before empire, where power was not with institutions or governments alone, where any owner or colonizer had the violent power of a ubiquitous state. This debt attached to those who through dumb insolence or nocturnal plans ran away without leaving, left without getting out. This debt got shared with anyone whose soul was sought for labor power, whose spirit was borne with a price marking it. And it is still shared, never credited and never abiding credit, a debt you play, a debt you walk, and debt you love. And without credit this debt is infinitely complex. It does not resolve in profit, seize assets, or balance in payment. The black radical tradition is the movement that works through this debt. The black radical tradition is debt work. It works in the bad debt of those in bad debt. It works intimately and at a distance until autonomia, for instance, remembers, and forgets. The black radical tradition is un-consolidated debt.

DEBT AND REFUGE

We went to the public hospital but it was private, but we went through the door marked 'private' to the nurses' coffee room, and it was public. We went to the public university but it was private, but we went to the barber shop on campus and it was public. We went into the hospital, into the university, into the library, into the park. We were offered credit for our debt. We were granted citizenship. We were given the credit of the state, the right to make private any public gone bad. Good citizens can match credit and debt. They get credit for knowing the difference, for knowing their place. Bad debt leads to bad publics, publics unmatched, unconsolidated, unprofitable. We were made honorary citizens. We honored our debt to the nation. We rated the service, scored the cleanliness, paid our fees.

Then we went to the barbershop and they gave us a Christmas breakfast, and we went to the coffee room and got coffee and red pills. We were going to run but we didn't have to. They ran. They ran across the state and across the economy, like a secret cut, a public outbreak, a fugitive fold. They ran but they didn't go anywhere. They stayed so we could stay. They saw our bad debt coming a mile off. They showed us this was the public, the real public, the fugitive public, and where to look for it. Look for it here where they say the state doesn't work. Look for it here where they say there is something wrong with that street. Look for it here where new policies are to be introduced. Look for it here where tougher measures are to be taken, bells are to be tightened, papers are to be served, neighborhoods are to be swept. Anywhere bad debt elaborates itself. Anywhere you can stay, conserve yourself, plan. A few minutes, a few days when you cannot hear them say there is something wrong with you.

DEBT AND GOVERNANCE

We hear them say, what's wrong with you is your bad debt. You're not working. You fail to pay your debt to society. You have no credit, but that is to be expected. You have bad credit, and that is fine. But bad debt is a problem. Debt seeking only other debt, detached from creditors, fugitive from restructuring. Destructuring debt, now that's wrong. But even still, what's wrong with you can be fixed. First we give you a chance. That's called governance, a chance to be interested, and a shot even at being disinterested. That's policy. Or we give you policy, if you are still wrong, still bad. Bad debt is senseless, which is to say it cannot be perceived by the senses of capital. But there is therapy available. Governance wants to connect your debt again to the outside world. You are on the spectrum, the capitalist spectrum of interests. You are the wrong end. Your bad debt looks unconnected, autistic, in its own world. But you can be developed. You can get credit after all. The key is interests. Tell us what you want. Tell us what you want and we can help you get it, on credit. We can lower the rate so you can have interest. We can raise the rate so you will pay attention. But we can't do it alone. Governance only works when you work, when you tell us your interests, when you invest your interests again in debt and credit. Governance is the therapy of your interests, and your interests will bring your credit back. You will have an investment, even in debt. And governance will gain new senses, new perceptions, new advances into the world of bad debt, new victories in the war on those without interests, those who will not speak for themselves, participate, identify their interests, invest, inform, demand credit.

Governance does not seek credit. It does not seek citizenship, although it is often understood to do so. Governance seeks debt, debt that will seek credit. Governance cannot not know what might be shared, what might be mutual, what might be common. Why award credit, why award citizenship? Only debt is productive, only debt makes credit possible, only debt lets credit rule. Productivity always comes before rule, even if the students of governance do not understand this, and even if governance itself barely understands this. But rule does come, and today it is called policy, the reign of precarity.

And who knows where it will hit you, some creditor walking by you. You keep your eyes down but he makes policy anyway, smashes any conservation you have built up, any bad debt you are smuggling. Your life goes back to vicious chance, to arbitrary violence, a new credit card, new car loan, torn from those who hid you, ripped from those who shared bad debt with you. They don't hear from you again.

STUDY AND PLANNING

The student has no interests. The student's interests must be identified, declared, pursued, assessed, counseled, and credited. Debt produces interests. The student will be indebted. The student will be interested. Interest the students! The student can be calculated by her debts, can calculate her debts with her interests. She is in sight of credit, in sight of graduation, in sight of being a creditor, of being invested in education, a citizen. The student with interests can demand policies, can formulate policy, give herself credit, pursue bad debtors with good policy, sound policy, evidence-based policy. The student with credit can privatize her own university. The student can start her own NGO, invite others to identify their interests, put them on the table, join the global conversation, speak for themselves, get credit, manage debt. Governance is interest-bearing. Credit and debt. There is no other definition of good governance, no other interest. The public and private in harmony, in policy, in pursuit of bad debt, on the trail of fugitive publics, chasing evidence of refuge. The student graduates.

But not all of them. Some still stay, committed to black study in the university's undercommon rooms. They study without an end, plan without a pause, rebel without a policy, conserve without a patrimony. They study in the university and the university forces them under, relegates them to the state of those without interests, without credit, without debt that bears interest, that earns credits. They never graduate. They just ain't ready. They're building something in there, something down there. Mutual debt, debt unpayable, debt unbounded, debt unconsolidated, debt to each other in a study group, to others in a nurses' room, to others in a barber shop, to others in a squat, a dump, a woods, a bed, an embrace.

And in the undercommons of the university they meet to elaborate their debt without credit, their debt without count, without interest, without repayment. Here they meet those others who dwell in a different compulsion, in the same debt, a distance, forgetting, remembered again but only after. These other ones carry bags of newspaper clippings, or sit at the end of the bar, or stand at the stove cooking, or sit on a box at the newsstand, or speak through bars, or speak in tongues. These other ones have a passion to tell you what they have found, and they are surprised you want to listen, even though they've been expecting you. Sometimes the story is not clear, or it starts in a whisper. It goes around again but listen, it is funny again, every time. This knowledge has been degraded, and the research rejected. They can't get access to books, and no one will publish them. Policy has concluded they are conspiratorial, heretical, criminal, amateur. Policy says they can't handle debt and will never get credit. But if you listen to them they will tell you: we will not handle credit, and we cannot handle debt, debt flows through us, and there's no time to tell you everything, so much bad debt, so much to forget and remember again. But if we listen to them they will say: come let's plan something together. And that's what we're going to do. We're telling all of you but we're not telling anyone else.

PLANNING AND POLICY

Let's get together, get some land
Raise our food, like the man
Save our money like the mob
Put up the factory on the job

James Brown, "Funky President"

The hope that Cornel West wrote about in 1984 was not destined to become what we call 'policy.' The ones who practiced it, within and against the grain of every imposed contingency, always had a plan. In and out of the depths of Reaganism, against the backdrop and by way of a resuscitory irruption into politics that Jesse Jackson could be said to have both symbolised and quelled, something West indexes as black radicalism, which "hopes against hope…in order to survive in the deplorable present," asserts a metapolitical surrealism that sees and sees through the evidence of mass incapacity, cutting the despair it breeds. Exuberantly metacritical hope has always exceeded every immediate circumstance in its incalculably varied everyday enactments of the fugitive art of social life. This art is practiced on and over the edge of politics, beneath its ground, in animative and improvisatory decomposition of its inert body. It emerges as an ensemblic stand, a kinetic set of positions, but also takes the form of embodied notation, study, score. Its encoded noise is hidden in plain sight from the ones who refuse to see and hear – even while placing under constant surveillance – the thing whose repressive imitation they call for and are. Now, more than a quarter century after West's analysis, and after an intervening iteration that had the nerve to call hope home while serially disavowing it and helping to extend and prepare its almost total eclipse, the remains of American politics exudes hope once again. Having seemingly lost its redoubled edge while settling in and for the carceral techniques of the possible, having thereby unwittingly become the privileged mode of expression of a kind of despair, hope appears now simply to be a matter of policy. Policy, on the other hand, now comes into view as no simple matter.

What we are calling policy is the new form command takes as command takes hold. It has been noted that with new uncertainties in how and where surplus value is generated, and how and where it will be generated next, economic mechanisms of compulsion have been replaced by directly political forms. Of course for the colonial subject this change is no change as Fanon understood; and as Nahum Chandler has pointed out, the problem of the color line is neither a matter of a new nor an old primitive accumulation. The problem is nothing other than the way the difference between labor and capital remains prior to its remainder and is made abundant or into abundance. Moreover what we are calling policy comes into view now not because management has failed in the workplace, where it proliferates as never before, but because economic management cannot win the battle that rages in the realm of social reproduction. Here management encounters forms of what we will call planning that resist its every effort to impose a compulsion of scarcity through seizing the means of social reproduction. In the undercommons of the social reproductive realm the means, which is to say the planners, are still part of the plan. And the plan is to invent the means in a common experiment launched from any kitchen, any back porch, any basement, any hall, any park bench, any improvised party, every night. This ongoing experiment with the informal, carried out by and on the means of social reproduction, as the to come of the forms of life, is what we mean by planning; planning in the undercommons is not an activity, not fishing or dancing or teaching or loving, but the ceaseless experiment with the futurial presence of the forms of life that make such activities possible. It is these means that were eventually stolen by, in having been willingly given up to, state socialism whose perversion of planning was a crime second only to the deployment of policy in today's command economy.

Of course, the old forms of command have never gone away. The carceral state is still in effect and strategic wars on drugs, youth, violence, and terrorism have even given way to logistic wars of drones and credit. But horrible as such state command remains, it now deputises and delegates its power to seemingly countless and utterly accountable and accounted for agents who perform contemporary internal versions of the knightriders and settlers of earlier state violence deputisations. Or rather, since nightriders and settlers never really went away, deputised for segregation, anti-communism, migration, and nuclear family heteropatriarchy in much of the Global North, what policy represents is a new weapon in the hands of these citizen-deputies. Stand your ground – because man was not born to run away, because his color won't run, because again and again the settler must incant the disavowal and target the epidermalised trace of his own desire for refuge – is only the most notorious iteration of this renewed dispersal and deputisation of state violence, aimed into the fugitive, ambling neighbourhoods of the undercommons.

Content neither with abandoning the realm of social reproduction nor conditioning it for the workplace, the two always related moves of the relative autonomy of the capitalist state, today capital wants in. It has glimpsed the value of social reproduction and wants control of the means, and no longer just by converting them into productivities within formal industrialisations of care, food, education, sex, etc. but by gaining access to and directly controlling the informal experiment with the social reproduction of life itself. To do this, it has to break up the ongoing plans of the undercommons. And here, with bitter irony, is where the hope West could still speak of in 1984, which has subsequently gone back underground, is conjured as an image whose fecklessness is also its monstrosity. What we talk about, in its survival, as planning appears, in its waning, as hope, which has been deployed against us in ever more perverted and reduced form by the Clinton-Obama axis for much of the last twenty years.

Planning is self-sufficiency at the social level, and it reproduces in its experiment not just what it needs, life, but what it wants, life in difference, in the play of the general antagonism. Planning starts from the solidity, the continuity, and the rest of this social self-sufficiency, though it does not end there in having placed all these complex motion. It begins, as this disruption of beginning, with what we might call a militant preservation. And these are its means. Policy deputises those willing to, those who come to want to, break up these means as a way of controlling them, as once it was necessary to de-skill a worker in a factory by breaking up his means of production. And it does this by diagnosing the planners. Policy says that those who plan have something wrong with them, something deeply – ontologically – wrong with them. This is the first thrust of policy as dispersed, deputised command. What's wrong with them? They won't change. They won't embrace change. They've lost hope. So say the policy deputies. They need to be given hope. They need to see that change is the only option. By change what the policy deputies mean is contingency, risk, flexibility, and adaptability to the groundless ground of the hollow capitalist subject, in the realm of automatic subjection that is capital. Policy is thus arrayed in the exclusive and exclusionary uniform/ity of contingency as imposed consensus, which both denies and at the very same time seeks to destroy the ongoing plans, the fugitive initiations, the black operations, of the multitude.

As resistance from above, policy is a new class phenomenon because the act of making policy for others, of pronouncing others as incorrect, is at the same time an audition for a post-fordist economy that deputies believe rewards those who embrace change but which, in reality, arrests them in contingency, flexibility, and that administered precarity that imagines itself to be immune from what Judith Butler might call our undercommon precariousness. This economy is powered by constant and automatic insistence upon the externalisation of risk, the placement at an externally imposed risk of all life, so that work against risk can be harvested without end.

Policy is the form that opportunism takes in this environment, as the embrace of the radically extra-economic, political character of command today. It is a demonstration of the will to contingency, the willingness to be made contingent and to make contingent all around you. It is a demonstration designed to separate you from others, in the interest of a universality reduced to private property that is not yours, that is the fiction of your own advantage. Opportunism sees no other way, has no alternative, but separates itself by its own vision, its ability to see the future of its own survival in this turmoil against those who cannot imagine surviving in this turmoil (even if they must do so all the time). The ones who survive the brutality of mere survival are said by policy to lack vision, to be stuck in an essentialist way of life, and, in the most extreme cases, to be without interests, on the one hand, and incapable of disinterestedness, on the other. Every utterance of policy, no matter its intent or content, is first and foremost a demonstration of one's ability to be close to the top in the hierarchy of the post-fordist economy.

As an operation from above designed to break up the means of social reproduction and make them directly productive for capital, policy must first deal with the fact that the multitude is already productive for itself. This productive imagination is its genius, its impossible, and nevertheless material, collective head. And this is a problem because plans are afoot, black operations are in effect, and in the undercommons all the organizing is done. The multitude uses every quiet moment, every sundown, every moment of militant preservation, to plan together, to launch, to compose (in) its surreal time. It is difficult for policy to deny these plans directly, to ignore these operations, to pretend that those who stay in motion need to stop and get a vision, to contend that base communities for escape need to believe in escape. And if this is difficult for policy then so too is the next and crucial step, instilling the value of radical contingency, instructing participation in change from above. Of course, some plans can be dismissed by policy – plans hatched darker than blue, on the criminal side, out of love. But most will instead require another approach to command.

So how does policy attempt to break this means, this militant preservation, all this planning? After the diagnosis that something is deeply wrong with the planners comes the prescription: help and correction. Policy will help. Policy will help with the plan and, even more, policy will correct the planners. Policy will discover what is not yet theorized, what is not yet fully contingent, and most importantly what is not yet legible. Policy is correction, forcing itself with mechanical violence upon the incorrect, the uncorrected, the ones who do not know to seek their own correction. Policy distinguishes itself from planning by distinguishing those who dwell in policy and fix things from those who dwell in planning and must be fixed. This is the first rule of policy. It fixes others. In an extension of Michel Foucault's work we might say of this first rule that its accompanying concern is with good government, with how to fix others in a position of equilibrium, even if today this requires constant recalibration. But the objects of this constant adjustment provoke this attention because they just don't want to govern, let alone be governed, at all. To break these means of planning, and so to determine them in recombined and privatized ways, is the necessary goal and instrumentality of policy as command. It wants to smash all forms of militant preservation, to break the movement of social rest – in which the next plan always remains potential – with a dream of settled potency. This is now what change means, what policy is for, as it invades the social reproductive realm where, as Leopaldina Fortunati noted three decades ago, the struggle rages.

And because such policy emerges materially from post-fordist opportunism, policy must optimally allow for each policy deputy to take advantage of his opportunity and fix others as others, as those who have not just made an error in planning (or indeed an error by planning) but who are themselves in error. And from the perspective of policy, of this post-fordist opportunism, there is indeed something wrong with those who plan together. They are out of joint – instead of constantly positing their position in contingency, they seek solidity in a mobile place from which to plan, some hold in which to imagine, some love on which to count. Again, this is not just a political problem from the point of view of policy, but an ontological one. Brushing the ground beneath their feet, finding anti- and ante-contingent flight in putting their feet on the ground, differences escape into their own outer depths signalling the problematic essentialism of those who think and act like they are something in particular, although at the same time that something is, from the perspective of policy, whatever they say it is, which is nothing in particular.

To get these planners out of this problem of essentialism, this choreographic fixity and repose, this security and base and bass-lined curve, they must come to imagine they can be more, they can do more, they can change, they can be changed. After all, they keep making plans and plans fail as a matter of policy. Plans must fail because planners must fail. Planners are static, essential, just surviving. They do not see clearly. They hear things. They lack perspective. They fail to see the complexity. To the deputies, planners have no vision, no real hope for the future, just a plan here and now, an actually existing plan.

They need hope. They need vision. They need to have their sights lifted above the furtive plans and night launches of their despairing lives. They need vision. Because from the perspective of policy it is too dark in there, in the black heart of the undercommons, to see. You can hear something, can feel something present at its own making. But the deputies can bring hope, and hope can lift planners and their plans, the means of social reproduction, above ground into the light, out of the shadows, away from these dark senses. Deputies fix others, not in an imposition upon but in the imposition of selves, as objects of control and command, whether one is posited as being capable of selfhood or not. Whether they lack consciousness or politics, utopianism or common sense, hope has arrived.

Having been brought to light and into their own new vision, planners will become participants. And participants will be taught to reject essence for contingency, as if planning and improvisation, flexibility and fixity, and complexity and simplicity, were opposed within an imposition there is no choice but to inhabit, as some exilic home where policy sequesters its own imagination, so they can be safe from one another. It is crucial that planners choose to participate. Policy is a mass effort. Intellectuals will write articles in the newspapers, philosophers will hold conferences on new utopias, bloggers will debate, and politicians will compromise here, where change is policy's only constant. Participating in change is the second rule of policy.

Now hope is an orientation toward this participation in change, this participation as change. This is the hope policy rolls like tear gas into the undercommons. Policy not only tries to impose this hope, but also enacts it. Those who dwell in policy do so not just by invoking contingency but by riding it, and so, in a sense, proving it. Those who dwell in policy are prepared. They are legible to change, liable to change, lendable to change. Policy is not so much a position as a disposition, a disposition toward display. This is why policy's chief manifestation is governance.

Governance should not be confused with government or governmentality. Governance is most importantly a new form of expropriation. It is the provocation of a certain kind of display, a display of interests as disinterestedness, a display of convertibility, a display of legibility. Governance is an instrumentalisation of policy, a set of protocols of deputisation, where one simultaneously auctions and bids on oneself, where the public and the private submit themselves to post-fordist production. Governance is the harvesting of the means of social reproduction but it appears as the acts of will, and therefore as the death drive, of the harvested. As capital cannot know directly the affect, thought, sociality, and imagination that make up the undercommon means of social reproduction, it must instead prospect for these in order to extract and abstract them as labor. That prospecting, which is the real bio-prospecting, seeks to break an integrity that has been militantly preserved. Governance, the voluntary but dissociative offering up of interests, willing participation in the general privacy and public privation, grants capital this knowledge, this wealth-making capacity. Policy emits this offering, violently manifest as a moral provocation. The ones who would correct and the ones who would be corrected converge around this imperative of submission that is played out constantly not only in that range of correctional facilities that Foucault analysed – the prisons, the hospitals, the asylums – but also in corporations, universities and NGOs. That convergence is given not only in the structures and affects of endless war but also in the brutal processes and perpetual processing of peace.

Governance, despite its own hopes for a universality of exclusion, is for the inducted, for those who know how to articulate interests disinterestedly, those who vote and know why they vote (not because someone is black or female but because he or she is smart), who have opinions and want to be taken seriously by serious people. In the mean time, policy must still pursue the quotidian sphere of open secret plans. Policy posits curriculum against study, child development against play, human capital against work. It posits having a voice against hearing voices, networked friending against contactual friendship. Policy posits the public sphere, or the counter-public sphere, or the black public sphere, against the illegal occupation of the illegitimately privatized.

Policy is not the one against the many, the cynical against the romantic, or the pragmatic against the principled. It is simply baseless vision, woven into settler's fabric. It is against all conservation, all rest, all gathering, cooking, drinking and smoking if they lead to marronage. Policy's vision is to break it up then fix it, move it along by fixing it, manufacture ambition and give it to your children. Policy's hope is that there will be more policy, more participation, more change. But there is also a danger in all this participation, a danger of crisis.

When those who plan together start to participate without first being fixed, this leads to crisis. Participation without fully entering the blinding light of this dim enlightenment, without fully functioning families and financial responsibility, without respect for the rule of law, without distance and irony, without submission to the rule of expertise; participation that is too loud, too fat, too loving, too full, too flowing, too dread; this leads to crisis. People are in crisis. Economies are in crisis. We are facing an unprecedented crisis, a crisis of participation, a crisis of faith. Is there any hope? Yes, there is, say the deputies, if we can pull together, if we can share a vision of change. For policy, any crisis in the productivity of radical contingency is a crisis in participation, which is to say, a crisis provoked by the wrong participation of the wrong(ed). This is the third rule of policy.

The crisis of the credit crunch caused by sub-prime debtors, the crisis of race in the 2008 US elections produced by Reverend Wright and Bernie Mac, the crisis in the Middle East produced by Hamas, the crisis of obesity produced by unhealthy eaters, the crisis of the environment produced by Chinese and Indians, are all instances of incorrect and uncorrected participation. The constant materialisation of planning in such participation is simply the inevitability of crisis, according to the deputised, who prescribe, as a corrective, hope for and hopefulness in correction. They say that participation must be hopeful, must have vision, must embrace change; that participants must be fashioned, in a general imposition of self-fashioning, as hopeful, visionary, change agents. Celebrating their freedom on lockdown in the enterprise zone, guarding that held contingency where the fashioning and correction of selves and others is always on automatic, the participant is the deputy's mirror image.

Deputies will lead the way toward concrete changes in the face of crisis. Be smart, they say. Believe in change. This is what we have been waiting for. Stop criticising and offer solutions. Set up roadblocks and offer workshops. Check ID's and give advice. Distinguish between the desire to correct and the desire to plan with others. Ruthlessly seek out and fearfully beware militant preservation, in an undercommons of means without ends, of love among things. Now's the time to declare and, in so doing, correctly fashion yourself as the one who is deputised to correct others. Now's the time, before its night again. Before you start singing another half-illiterate fantasy. Before you resound that ongoing amplification of the bottom, the operations on the edge of normal rhythm's soft center. Before someone says let's get together and get some land. But we're not smart. We plan. We plan to stay, to stick and move. We plan to be communist about communism, to be unreconstructed about reconstruction, to be absolute about abolition, here, in that other, undercommon place, as that other, undercommon thing, that we preserve by inhabiting. Policy can't see it, policy can't read it, but it's intelligible if you got a plan.

FANTASY IN THE HOLD

LOGISTICS, OR THE SHIPPING

To work today is to be asked, more and more, to do without thinking, to feel without emotion, to move without friction, to adapt without question, to translate without pause, to desire without purpose, to connect without interruption. Only a short time ago many of us said work went through the subject to exploit our social capacities, to wring more labor power from our labor. The soul descended onto the shop floor as Franco 'Bifo' Berardi wrote, or ascended like a virtuoso speaker without a score as Paolo Virno suggested. More prosaically we heard the entrepreneur, the artist, and the stakeholder all proposed as new models of subjectivity conducive to channeling the general intellect. But today we are prompted to ask: why worry about the subject at all, why go through such beings to reach the general intellect? And why limit production to subjects, who are after all such a small part of the population, such a small history of mass intellectuality? There have always been other ways to put bodies to work, even to maintain the fixed capital of such bodies, as Christian Marrazi might say. And anyway for capital the subject has become too cumbersome, too slow, too prone to error, too controlling, to say nothing of too rarified, too specialized a form of life. Yet it is not we who ask this question. This is the automatic, insistent, driving question of the field of logistics. Logistics wants to dispense with the subject altogether. This is the dream of this newly dominant capitalist science. This is the drive of logistics and the algorithms that power that dream, the same algorithmic research that Donald Rumsfeld was in fact quoting in his ridiculed unknown unknowns speech, a droning speech that announced the conception of a drone war. Because drones are not un-manned to protect American pilots. They are un-manned because they think too fast for American pilots.

Today this field of logistics is in hot pursuit of the general intellect in its most concrete form, that is its potential form, its informality, when any time and any space and any thing could happen, could be the next form, the new abstraction. Logistics is no longer content with diagrams or with flows, with calculations or with predictions. It wants to live in the concrete itself in space at once, time at once, form at once. We must ask where it got this ambition and how it could come to imagine it could dwell in or so close to the concrete, the material world in its informality, the thing before there is anything. How does it proposes to dwell in nothing, and why?

The rise of logistics is rapid. Indeed, to read today in the field of logistics is to read a booming field, a conquering field. In military science and in engineering of course, but also in business studies, in management research, logistics is everywhere. And beyond these classic capitalist sciences, its ascent is echoed ahistorically in the emerging fields of object-oriented philosophy and cognitive neuroscience, where the logistical conditions of knowledge production go unnoticed, but not the effects. In military science the world has been turned upside down. Traditionally strategy led and logistics followed. Battle plans dictated supply lines. No more. Strategy, traditional ally and partner of logisitics, is today increasingly reduced to collateral damage in the drive of logistics for dominance. In war without end, war without battles, only the ability to keep fighting, only logistics, matters.

And so too business innovation has become logistical and no longer strategic. Business innovation of course does not come from business. It is more often derived from military strategies of resistance to its own armies, transferred free to business. Once this consisted in transferring innovations like the line and the formation and the chain of command from military science to the factory and the office, or transferring psychological and propaganda warfare to human relations and marketing. These were free transfers of strategic innovation, requiring managers to instantiate and maintain them. No more. As everything from the internet to the shipping container testify, in keeping with cold wars and wars on terror that lead always to the failure of strategy, it is logistical free transfers that matter. Containerisation was failing as a business innovation until the American government used containers to try to supply its troops in South East Asia with enough weapons, booze, and drugs to keep them from killing their own officers, to keep a war going that could not be won strategically. Those who dreamt of the internet, if not those who built it, were precisely worried about the corruption of intelligence that the outbreak of democracy, as the Trilateral Commission thought of it, made possible in the 1970s. ARPANET as an intelligence gathering network could not have its head turned by sex or ideology, much less the powerful combination of the two. It would not be confused by the outbreak of democracy. And it assumed a never-ending accumulation of intelligence for a never-ending war that many would not want to fight. To Toni Negri's challenge, show me a business innovation and I will show you a worker's rebellion, we could add a pre-history the state fearing its own workforce.

Containerisation itself stands for what should be called the first wave of regulatory innovation as logistics, which moves in tandem with the first wave of financialisation, the other response to these insurgencies by capitalism, aside from violent repression. Indeed logistics and financialisation worked together in both phases of innovation, with, roughly speaking, the first working on production across bodies, the second renovating the subject of production. Financialisation is perhaps the better known of the two strategies of resistance to rebellion, with a first phase selling off factories and state assets, and the second selling of homes and banks, only in both instances to rent them back on credit in a kind of global pawn-broking. This had the desired effect of reorganizing any subjects attached to such pawned objects into walking, talking credit reports, who contract their own financial contagion, as Randy Martin and Angela Mitropoulos suggest in different ways, eventually producing an entity hooked into financial affects in a way that make it more logistical object than strategic subject.

But all the while logistics itself had no lasting interest in this financialised subject or its reorganization. Logistics was after a bigger prize, something that has always haunted it but became more palpable in the double wave that produced logistical populations when the container came to rule the waves, the roads, and the rails with information, affect, meaning shot through flesh as through other objects, again on a scale and in a form impossible to ignore. The prize seemed almost within reach. Of course this fantasy of what Marx called the automatic subject, this fantasy that capital could exist without labor, is nothing new but is continually explored at the nexus of finance capital, logistics and the terror of state-sponsored personhood which is instantiated in various pageants of conferral and withholding. It is marked today by the term human capital. Human capital would appear to be a strategic category, involved as Michel Feher suggests, with a strategy of investment in and speculation on the self. But as Marina Vishmidt reminds us, the automatic subject of capital that human capital seeks to emulate, is a hollow subject, and a subject dedicated to hollowing itself precisely by expelling the negativity of labor, by exiling the one who, in being less and more than one, are his figure, his other, his double, the bearers of a generativity without reserve. Now, human capital is the automatic subject's substitute, carrying out its engagement with the skills of daily financialisation and logistics, both of which act on it as if it were an impediment to movement and not a vehicle in motion. Human capital, in other words, departs from the strategic subject of neoliberalism, generalizing through self-infliction the departure that subject ritually imposes upon its exiled interiors and making of itself a porous object that still talks like a subject, as if in some burlesque enactment of philosophy's dream of the ultimate reconciliation. It is for this reason that human capital cannot be strategized, or indeed managed, in any traditional sense, and therefore in turn we can see the hollowing out of the field of business strategy, including the decline of the MBA degree, and the rise of 'leadership studies.' Leadership studies weighs down the bookstore shelves and the business student today but leadership cannot manage.

It is the evacuation of management by strategy in a desperate attempt to maintain control of private gain from a form of social production under capital that is becoming automatic and therefore not so much unmanageable as auto-managed. What is opened up here is a course in and for a general logistics. To read logistics is to read of the stated desire to be rid of what logistics calls 'the controlling agent,' to free the flow of goods from 'human time' and 'human error.' The greedy algorithm of the traveling salesman still requires strategic intervention because it cannot evolve as new problems emerge, unless one counts as evolution the capacity to destroy, or the incapacity that allows the self-destruction, of the contained. It cannot solve, for instance, the Canadian traveller problem, where roads disappear under snow producing new problems for the most efficient movement of the trucks. Here is where the evolutionary and genetic algorithms enter often in more Lamarckian than Darwinian clothing. But one thing is agreed. Strategy is now blocking the road as surely as snow blocks the road to Sudbury. For logistics, the subject of whatever, as Michael Hardt calls it, must yield to the object of whatever. Logistical populations will be created to do without thinking, to feel without emotion, to move without friction, to adapt without question, to translate without pause, to connect without interruption, or they will be dismantled and disabled as bodies in the same way they are assembled, by what Patricia Clough calls population racism. From here, logistics is master of all that it surveys.

But what might look like smooth sailing, flat waters, flat being, is not so undisturbed. Uncertainty surrounds the holding of things and in a manner that Luciana Parisi describes, in which the algorithm generates it own critique, logistics discovers too late that the sea has no back door. And it is not just the class of greedoids, the possessive individuals of the algorithmic world, but these new genetic and evolutionary algorithms too, whose very premise is that there must be something more, something in what they have grasped that remains beyond their reach. These algorithms are defined by what they are not yet, and what they can never fully become, despite the dreams of their materialist eugenicists. Every attempt by logistics to dispel strategy, to banish human time, to connect without going through the subject, to subject without handling things, resists something that was already resisting it, namely the resistance that founds modern logistics. Concerned to move objects and move through objects, logistics removes itself from the informality that founds its objects and itself. There is some/thing logistics is always after.

LOGISTICALITY, OR THE SHIPPED

Where did logistics get this ambition to connect bodies, objects, affects, information, without subjects, without the formality of subjects, as if it could reign sovereign over the informal, the concrete and generative indeterminacy of material life? The truth is, modern logistics was born that way. Or more precisely it was born in resistance to, given as the acquisition of, this ambition, this desire and this practice of the informal. Modern logistics is founded with the first great movement of commodities, the ones that could speak. It was founded in the Atlantic slave trade, founded against the Atlantic slave. Breaking from the plundering accumulation of armies to the primitive accumulation of capital, modern logistics was marked, branded, seared with the transportation of the commodity labor that was not, and ever after would not be, no matter who was in that hold or containerized in that ship. From the motley crew who followed in the red wakes of these slave ships, to the prisoners shipped to the settler colonies, to the mass migrations of industrialisation in the Americas, to the indentured slaves from India, China, and Java, to the trucks and boats leading north across the Mediterranean or the Rio Grande, to one-way tickets from the Philippines to the Gulf States or Bangladesh to Singapore, logistics was always the transport of slavery, not 'free' labor. Logistics remains, as ever, the transport of objects that is held in the movement of things. And the transport of things remains, as ever, logistics' unrealizable ambition.

Logistics could not contain what it had relegated to the hold. It cannot. Robert F. Harney, the historian of migration 'from the bottom-up,' used to say once you crossed the Atlantic, you were never on the right side again. B Jenkins, a migrant sent by history, used to turn a broken circle in the basement floor to clear the air when welcoming her students, her panthers. No standpoint was enough, no standpoint was right. She and their mothers and fathers tilled the same fields, burned up the same desert roads, preoccupied the same merely culinary union. Harney kept in mind the mass migrations from Southern and Eastern Europe at the turn of the 19th century, beside themselves in the annunciation of logistical modernity. No standpoint. If commodity labor would come to have a standpoint, the standpoint from which one's own abolition became necessary, then what of those who had already been abolished and remained? If the proletariat was located at a point in the circuits of capital, a point in the production process from which it had a peculiar view of capitalist totality, what of those who were located at every point, which is to say at no point, in the production process? What of those who were not just labor but commodity, not just in production but in circulation, not just in circulation but in distribution as property, not just property but property that reproduced and realized itself? The standpoint of no standpoint, everywhere and nowhere, of never and to come, of thing and nothing. If the proletariat was thought capable of blowing the foundations sky high, what of the shipped, what of the containerized? What could such flesh do? Logistics somehow knows that it is not true that we do not yet know what flesh can do. There is a social capacity to instantiate again and again the exhaustion of the standpoint as undercommon ground that logistics knows as unknowable, calculates as an absence that it cannot have but always longs for, that it cannot, but longs, to be or, at least, to be around, to surround. Logisitics senses this capacity as never before – this historical insurgent legacy, this historicity, this logisticality, of the shipped.

Modernity is sutured by this hold. This movement of things, unformed objects, deformed subjects, nothing yet and already. This movement of nothing is not just the origin of modern logistics, but the annunciation of modernity itself, and not just the annunciation of modernity itself but the insurgent prophesy that all of modernity will have at its heart, in its own hold, this movement of things, this interdicted, outlawed social life of nothing. The work of Sandro Mazzadra and

Brett Neilson on borders for instance reminds us that the proliferation of borders between states, within states, between people, within people is a proliferation of states of statelessness. These borders grope their way toward the movement of things, bang on containers, kick at hostels, harass camps, shout after fugitives, seeking all the time to harness this movement of things, this logisticality. But this fails to happen, borders fail to cohere, because the movement of things will not cohere. This logisticality will not cohere. It is, as Sara Ahmed says, queer disorientation, the absence of coherence, but not of things, in the moving presence of absolutely nothing. As Frank B. Wilderson III teaches us, the improvisational imperative is, therefore, "to stay in the hold of the ship, despite my fantasies of flight."

But this is to say that there are flights of fantasy in the hold of the ship. The ordinary fugue and fugitive run of the language lab, black phonography's brutally experimental venue. Paraontological totality is in the making. Present and unmade in presence, blackness is an instrument in the making. *Quasi una fantasia* in its paralegal swerve, its mad-worked braid, the imagination produces nothing but exsense in the hold. Do you remember the days of slavery? Nathaniel Mackey rightly says "The world was ever after/elsewhere,/no/way where we were/was there." No way where we are is here. Where we were, where we are, is what we meant by "mu," which Wilderson would rightly call "the void of our subjectivity." And so it is we remain in the hold, in the break, as if entering again and again the broken world, to trace the visionary company and join it. This contrapuntal island, where we are marooned in search of marronage, where we linger in stateless emergency, in our our lysed cell and held dislocation, our blown standpoint and lyred chapel, in (the) study of our sea-born variance, sent by its pre-history into arrivance without arrival, as a poetics of lore, of abnormal articulation, where the relation between joint and flesh is the folded distance of a musical moment that is emphatically, palpably imperceptible and, therefore, difficult to describe. Having defied degradation the moment becomes a theory of the moment, of the feeling of a presence that is ungraspable in the way that it touches. This musical moment – the moment of advent, of nativity in all its terrible beauty, in the alienation that is always already born in and as *parousia*

– is a precise and rigorous description/theory of the social life of the shipped, the terror of enjoyment in its endlessly redoubled folds. If you take up the hopelessly imprecise tools of standard navigation, the deathly reckoning of difference engines, maritime clocks and tables of damned assurance, you might stumble upon such a moment about two and a half minutes into "Mutron," a duet by Ed Blackwell and Don Cherry recorded in 1982. You'll know the moment by how it requires you to think the relation between fantasy and nothingness: what is mistaken for silence is, all of a sudden, transubstantial. The brutal interplay of advent and chamber demands the continual instigation of flown, recursive imagining; to do so is to inhabit an architecture and its acoustic, but to inhabit as if in an approach from outside; not only to reside in this unlivability but also to discover and enter it. Mackey, in the preface to his unbearably beautiful *Splay Anthem*, outlining the provenance and relationship between the book's serial halves ("Each was given its impetus by a piece of recorded music from which it takes its title, the Dogon 'Song of the Andoumboulou,' in one case, Don Cherry's [and Ed Blackwell's] *'Mu' First Part* and *'Mu' Second Part* in the other") speaks of mu in relation to a circling or spiraling or ringing, this roundness or rondo linking beginning and end, and to the wailing that accompanies entrance into and expulsion from sociality. But his speaking makes you wonder if music, which is not only music, is mobilized in the service of an eccentricity, a centrifugal force whose intimation Mackey also approaches, marking sociality's ecstatic existence beyond beginning and end, ends and means, out where one becomes interested in things, in a certain relationship between thingliness and nothingness and blackness that plays itself out in unmapped, unmappable, undercommon consent and consensuality. Blackness is the site where absolute nothingness and the world of things converge. Blackness is fantasy in the hold and Wilderson's access to it is in that he is one who has nothing and is, therefore, both more and less than one. He is the shipped. We are the shipped, if we choose to be, if we elect to pay an unbearable cost that is inseparable from an incalculable benefit.

How would you recognize the antiphonal accompaniment to gratuitous violence – the sound that can be heard as if it were in response to that violence, the sound that must be heard as that to which such violence responds? The answer, the unmasking, is mu not simply because in its imposed opposition to something, nothing is understood simply to veil, as if some epidermal livery, (some higher) being and is therefore relative as opposed to what Nishida Kitaro, would call absolute; but because nothing (this paraontological interplay of blackness and nothingness, this aesthetic sociality of the shipped, this logisticality) remains unexplored, because we don't know what we mean by it, because it is neither a category for ontology nor for socio-phenomenological analysis. What would it be for this to be understood in its own improper refusal of terms, from the exhausted standpoint that is not and that is not its own? "We attach," Fanon says, "a fundamental importance to the phenomenon of language and consequently consider the study of language essential for providing us with one element in understanding the black man's dimension of being-for-others, it being understood that to speak is to exist absolutely for the other." He says, moreover, that "[t]he black man possesses two dimensions: one with his fellow Blacks, the other with the Whites." But this is not simply a question of perspective, since what we speak of is this radical being beside itself of blackness, its off to the side, off on the inside, out from the outside imposition. The standpoint, the home territory, *chez lui* – Markman's off the mark, blind but insightful, mistranslation is illuminative, *among his own*, signifying a relationality that displaces the already displaced impossibility of home. Can this being together in homelessness, this interplay of the refusal of what has been refused, this undercommon appositionality, be a place from which emerges neither self-consciousness nor knowledge of the other but an improvisation that proceeds from somewhere on the other side of an unasked question? Not simply to be among his own; but to be among his own in dispossession, to be among the ones who cannot own, the ones who have nothing and who, in having nothing, have everything. This is the sound of an unasked question. A choir versus acquisition, chant and moan and *Sprechgesang*, babel and babble and gobbledygook, relaxin' by a brook or creek in Camarillo, singing to it, singing of it, singing with it, for the bird of the crooked beak, the generative hook of *le petit negre*, the little nigger's comic spear, the cosmic crook of language, the burnin' and lootin' of pidgin, Bird's talk, Bob's talk, bard talk, bar talk, baby talk, B talk, preparing the minds of the little negro steelworkers for meditation. Come on, get to this hard, serial information, this brutally beautiful medley of carceral intrication, this patterning of holds and what is held in the holds' phonic vicinity. That spiraling Mackey speaks of suffers brokenness and crumpling, the imposition of irrationally rationalized angles, compartments bearing nothing but breath and battery in hunted, haunted, ungendered intimacy. Is there a kind of propulsion, through compulsion, against the mastery of one's own speed, that ruptures both recursion and advance? What is the sound of this patterning? What does such apposition look like? What remains of eccentricity after the relay between loss and restoration has its say or song? In the absence of amenity, in exhaustion, there's a society of friends where everything can fold in dance to black, in being held and flown, in what was never silence. Can't you hear them whisper one another's touch?

HAPTICALITY, OR LOVE

Never being on the right side of the Atlantic is an unsettled feeling, the feeling of a thing that unsettles with others. It's a feeling, if you ride with it, that produces a certain distance from the settled, from those who determine themselves in space and time, who locate themselves in a determined history. To have been shipped is to have been moved by others, with others. It is to feel at home with the homeless, at ease with the fugitive, at peace with the pursued, at rest with the ones who consent not to be one. Outlawed, interdicted, intimate things of the hold, containerized contagion, logistics externalises logic itself to reach you, but this is not enough to get at the social logics, the social poesis, running through logisticality.

Because while certain abilities – to connect, to translate, to adapt, to travel – were forged in the experiment of hold, they were not the point. As David Rudder sings, "how we vote is not how we party." The hold's terrible gift was to gather dispossessed feelings in common, to create a new feel in the undercommons. Previously, this kind of feel was only an exception, an aberration, a shaman, a witch, a seer, a poet amongst others, who felt through others, through other things. Previously, except in these instances, feeling was mine or it was ours. But in the hold, in the undercommons of a new feel, another kind of feeling became common. This form of feeling was not collective, not given to decision, not adhering or reattaching to settlement, nation, state, territory or historical story; nor was it repossessed by the group, which could not now feel as one, reunified in time and space. No, when Black Shadow sings "are you feelin' the feelin?" he is asking about something else. He is asking about a way of feeling through others, a feel for feeling others feeling you. This is modernity's insurgent feel, its inherited caress, its skin talk, tongue touch, breath speech, hand laugh. This is the feel that no individual can stand, and no state abide. This is the feel we might call hapticality.

Hapticality, the touch of the undercommons, the interiority of sentiment, the feel that what is to come is here. Hapticality, the capacity to feel though others, for others to feel through you, for you to feel them feeling you, this feel of the shipped is not regulated, at least not successfully, by a state, a religion, a people, an empire, a piece of land, a totem. Or perhaps we could say these are now recomposed in the wake of the shipped. To feel others is unmediated, immediately social, amongst us, our thing, and even when we recompose religion, it comes from us, and even when we recompose race, we do it as race women and men. Refused these things, we first refuse them, in the contained, amongst the contained, lying together in the ship, the boxcar, the prison, the hostel. Skin, against epidermalisation, senses touching. Thrown together touching each other we were denied all sentiment, denied all the things that were supposed to produce sentiment, family, nation, language, religion, place, home. Though forced to touch and be touched, to sense and be sensed in that space of no space, though refused sentiment, history and home, we feel (for) each other.

A feel, a sentiment with its own interiority, there on skin, soul no longer inside but there for all to hear, for all to move. Soul music is a medium of this interiority on the skin, its regret the lament for broken hapticality, its self-regulatory powers the invitation to build sentimentality together again, feeling each other again, how we party. This is our hapticality, our love. This is love for the shipped, love as the shipped.

There's a touch, a feel you want more of, which releases you. The closest Marx ever got to the general antagonism was when he said "from each according to his ability, to each according to his need" but we have read this as the possession of ability and the possession of need. What if we thought of the experiment of the hold as the absolute fluidity, the informality, of this condition of need and ability? What if ability and need were in constant play and we found someone who dispossessed us so that this movement was our inheritance. Your love makes me strong, your love makes me weak. What if "the between the two," the lost desire, the articulation, was this rhythm, this inherited experiment of the shipped in the churning waters of flesh and expression that could grasp by letting go ability and need in constant recombination. If he moves me, sends me, sets me adrift in this way, amongst us in the undercommons. So long as she does this, she does not have to be.

Who knows where Marx got this inheritance of the hold, from Aristotle denying his slave world or Kant talking to sailors or Hegel's weird auto-eroticism or just being ugly and dark and fugitive. Like Zimmy says, precious angel, you know both our forefathers were slaves, which is not something to be ironic about. This feel is the hold that lets go (let's go) again and again to dispossess us of ability, fill us with need, give us ability to fill need, this feel. We hear the godfather and the old mole calling us to become, in whatever years we have, philosophers of the feel.

Love,
S/F

THE GENERAL ANTAGONISM:
AN INTERVIEW WITH
STEVPHEN SHUKAITIS

STEVPHEN: I'd like to start our conversation in a somewhat playful, metaphoric manner, with an idea from Selma James that I recently came across. Selma was describing the advice that CLR James gave her for writing: that she should keep a shoebox, collecting in it various ideas and thoughts. When the shoebox was getting filled she would have all that was needed for writing. If you were to introduce someone to your collaborative work through the form of a conceptual shoebox, what would be in it? What would be in there?

FRED: The thing I felt when I read that was, if I were Selma James, I would ask to get clarification on what he meant. The one thing I do that's similar is that I carry around little notebooks and I jot things down all the time. If I don't have my notebooks, I write notes on pieces of paper and stick them in my pocket. What's funny is that I don't think of it as a shoebox, because 95% of the time I write stuff down and that's the end of it. It's more that I have a thought and I write it down and then I never think about it again. Seldom do I even transcribe into the computer.

The one thing that I was interested in about the question, it strikes me, especially in thinking about working collaboratively, with Stefano, you sort of don't need a shoebox in a way, because I always feel like, when I'm asleep, he's up thinking about something. And also, working so closely with my wife, Laura, it's not as much having a shoebox in which I'm writing down my thoughts as that I'm having a long conversation with a few people. What I'm trying to say is that the content of the box is less important for me than the ongoing process of talking with somebody else, and the ideas that emerge. So, I don't feel like there are five or six ideas that I'm always working on and thinking about that I can pull out of my box. It's more like there are five or six people that I'm always thinking with. If you ask me, I couldn't tell you, 'oh there are these four or five ideas that I'm constantly going back to that I have to have in my box.' It doesn't feel that way. It feels more like there are one or two things that I've been talking about with people forever. And the conversation develops over the course of time, and you think of new things and you say new things. But, the ideas that are stuck in my head are usually things that somebody else said.

STEFANO: It's hard for me to answer because I'm a person who doesn't make notes on what I read, because I just know I'm not going to go back to them. I'm not a collector in that way. But, I also feel like there's something there; it's not necessarily a box, but perhaps as Fred says, a series of conversations. What's also interesting to me is that the conversations themselves can be discarded, forgotten, but there's something that goes on beyond the conversations which turns out to be the actual project. It's the same thing I think in the building of any kind of partnership or collectivity: it's not the thing that you do; it's the thing that happens while you're doing it that becomes important, and the work itself is some combination of the two modes of being. Or to put it in the way of *the shipped*, it's not the box that's important but the experiment among the *un/contained*.

STEVPHEN: Perhaps the shoebox metaphor was more useful for Selma in the sense that she was more cut off from social contact and was trying to write by herself, and trying to think in isolation, which has its own risks and downfalls. Reading through the texts you've written together, there is a certain set of concepts that you both develop and work with in ways that are somewhat idiosyncratic – perhaps they are the products of this ongoing dialogue that you have had for years, can you explain how these particular concepts have emerged from that?

STEFANO: I could list for you some of our concepts such as 'under-commons' or 'planning' or the ones we've been working with lately, around unsettling and the shipped. But, in a way, I feel like what I'm exploring with Fred, and what I would explore in other situations which aren't as developed but have been tried, for instance, with the collective at Queen Mary, University of London, is this: the concepts are ways to develop a mode of living together, a mode of being together that cannot be shared as a model but as an instance. So, I feel more like an 'idea thief' around this, as Guattari would say – I am hacking concepts and squatting terms as a way to help us do something. Which is not to say that we don't spend a lot of time developing and trying to make sense of these concepts or trying to figure out how new situations or circumstances might lead us to want to continue the concept, or on the other hand to say the term is no longer sufficient for what we're trying to say here. I'm thinking recently about some stuff that Fred wrote in response to a question of whether the occupations of the Occupy Movement could be understood to be doing something that we were calling 'planning.' And Fred said, "yeah, not just planning but also study and also what you may even call 'black study.'" So that for me was an example of where the concepts were letting us continue to move through different situations. In that sense I suppose they are there for us in some ways, even if I don't think of them as conceptual in the same way that maybe you would think of concepts more traditionally in philosophy where you have to make a system of them.

FRED: I think that's right. I feel, in a lot of ways, the fun thing about working collaboratively with someone is that you literally come to terms together. Stefano will point to different things he's read that I haven't read, different kinds of experiences that he's gone through. He'll take a term that I would never have thought of myself and I'll find myself totally drawn to the term and want to work with it. There will be other times when I'll want to do something to the term.

A metaphor popped into my head. You can either talk about it as having a kind of toolbox or also talk about it as having a kind of toy-box. With my kids, most of what they do with toys is turn them into props. They are constantly involved in this massive project of pretending. And the toys that they have are props for their pretending. They don't play with them the right way – a sword is what you hit a ball with and a bat is what you make music with. I feel that way about these terms. In the end what's most important is that the thing is put in play. What's most important about play is the interaction. One time we were driving in the car and my kids were playing this game called 'family,' and it's basically that they've created an alternative family and they just talk about what the alternative family is doing. This time, when they had really started enjoying the game, my eldest son looked at me, I could see him through the rearview mirror, and he said, "dad, we have a box, and we're going to let you open this box, and if you open the box, you can enter into our world." That's kind of what it feels like: there are these props, these toys, and if you pick them up you can move into some new thinking and into a new set of relations, a new way of being together, thinking together. In the end, it's the new way of being together and thinking together that's important, and not the tool, not the prop. Or, the prop is important only insofar as it allows you to enter; but once you're there, it's the relation and the activity that's really what you want to emphasize. So, with that said, if somebody's reading our stuff, and they think they can get something out of the term 'planning' or 'undercommons' or 'logisticality,' that's great, but what matters is what they do with it; it's where they take it in their own relations. When people read their stuff it leads people to look up and read ours. That also creates a different kind of relation between us, even if we're not necessarily cognizant of it.

STEFANO: Just pick up a toy...

STEVPHEN: Following on from that I'd like to ask something about how you approach writing together. If concepts are tools for living or toyboxes for playing, when you pick up a text that's finished, unless you've got some special texts that I don't know of, you don't get a sense of the playing or the living usually. What you get a sense of is some finished product where the collectivity animating the work that preceded it – which I would agree with you is the most important thing – somehow gets lost along the way. How do you negotiate that? Or is there a way to flag up, in a written text, "don't take this too seriously, go out and play with it"?

STEFANO: Well, one way that I do that is by revising how I say things. So, some people might call my style repetitive, partly because I'm re-phrasing things all the time, but also because I'm trying to show that I'm playing with something rather than that it's finished. If I'm going along in a kind of 'duh dum duh dum duh dum' rhyming kind of way in the writing, it's partly to say that we're in rehearsal here. And since we're rehearsing, you might as well pick up an instrument too. So, for me, it must be right there in the writing in some form. It's not enough to signal it outside the writing, to send the piece out and to say, 'oh, really this is still open for this or that.' It has to be somehow in the writing itself that the thing hasn't closed off. Part of that is that to write with another person is, in a sense, always to keep something open, because you always have the question of, "do they both think that way, who said that?" Instead of worrying about that, I think that's nice. That means that the text is already open to more than one, in that sense.

FRED: I think that's right. Sometimes, when you're listening to some-body, and you're trying to think about who's on the left channel and who's on the right channel. And then you kind of realize that it's not really that important. You spend all this time trying to figure it out, but then you realize that there's also this interaction and interplay that's still going on in the text. It's not a dead thing. What you lis-ten to or what you're reading is still moving and still living. It's still forming.

There's this thing I was trying to think about last year, teaching *Black Skin, White Masks,* and reading it and recognizing, finally, because I guess I'm kinda slow, that, "ah shit, Fanon went to medical school. This is important." Then to be fascinated by Fanon's use of the term '*lyse*,' lysis. He didn't write 'critique' or even 'analysis' but invoked this biochemical process of the breakdown of cells, which, then, experi-mentalists try to replicate. All of a sudden, reading Fanon means try-ing to find out what biochemists mean when they say 'lysis'. What might a doctor mean? Then recalling that Plato has a dialogue called *Lysis* that turns and keeps turning on what's interminable in the analysis or theory of friendship. Fanon's text is still open and it still opens. Now you have to go inside it. When you're inside, now, you have to go outside of it. Actually, you're being blown out of it – this happens within the context of a single authored piece when you realize it's not a single authored piece. Yeah, it's under his name, and one might say, of course that what I'm saying is not only simple and true but also mundane. Anybody who understands anything about reading will come to know this; "yeah, that's intertextuality." But, there's another way to think about it that lets you realize that it's even deeper than that. It's not just the simple fact of intertextuality that you're talking about. It's different. Recognizing that text is intertext is one thing. Seeing that a text is a social space is another. It's a deeper way of looking at it. To say that it's a social space is to say that stuff is going on: people, things, are meeting there and interacting, rubbing off one another, brushing against one another – and you enter into that social space, to try to be part of it. So, what I guess I'm trying to say is that the terms are important insofar as they allow you, or invite you, or propel you, or require you, to enter into that social space. But once you enter into that social space, terms are just one part of it, and there's other stuff too. There are things to do, places to go, and people to see in reading and writing – and it's about maybe even trying to figure out some kind of ethically responsible way to be in that world with other things.

Our first collaborations were in poetry. That's basically the better way to put it. All of that other stuff that I was just saying which made no sense: strike that! We've been thinking about stuff to do. Hanging around, talking, and drinking. Eventually things deteriorated to the point where we were writing something. But the collaboration is way older than the production of any text. The first thing we wrote together, "Doing Academic Labor," was in 90-something. I don't know. But there were fifteen years of hanging out together before we published something. Hopefully, when the last thing gets published, we'll have fifteen more years of hanging out together after that.

STEFANO: And then the next publication... [laughs]. The one thing that I was thinking about as you were talking about the text being a social space is it's exciting for me when we get to that point where the text is open enough that instead of being studied, it actually becomes the occasion for study. So, we enter into the social world of study, which is one in which you start to lose track of your debts and begin to see that the whole point is to lose track of them and just build them in a way that allows for everyone to feel that she or he can contribute or not contribute to being in a space. That seems to me to be not about saying there's no longer somebody who might have insisted or persisted in getting us into that time-space of study, but rather that the text is one way for that kind of insistence on study to be an open insistence, to be one that doesn't have to be about authority or ongoing leadership or anything like that, but a kind of invitation for other people to pick stuff up. I've been thinking more and more of study as something not where everybody dissolves into the student, but where people sort of take turns doing things for each other or for the others, and where you allow yourself to be possessed by others as they do something. That also is a kind of dispossession of what you might otherwise have been holding onto, and that possession is released in a certain way voluntarily, and then some other possession occurs by others.

I think that this notion also applies in the social space of the text itself, even where the study is not yet apparent. If you think about the way we read a text, we come in and out of it at certain moments, and those moments of possession are, for me, opportunities to say, well, how could this become more generalized? This sense of dispossession, and possession by the dispossessed is a way to think what Fred and I call the general antagonism, which is a concept that runs through all our work, as it runs through our sense of the world. The riotous production of difference which is the general antagonism cannot be tamed either by the feudal authority or social violence that is capitalism much less by policy initiatives like agonistic dialogues or alternative public spheres. But where the aim is not to suppress the general antagonism but to experiment with its informal capacity, that place is the undercommons or rather, whereever and whenever that experiment is going on within the general antagonism the undercommons is found. Being possessed by the dispossessed, and offering up possession through dispossession, is such an experiment and is, among other things, a way to think of love, and this too can arise in study. I think this is the kind of experiment we are attempting with the School for Study.

STEVPHEN: Preparing for the interview I resorted to a typically web 2.0 approach of asking on Facebook what questions I should ask. I sent some of these to you. One question that seemed quite interesting was whether it was possible to be part of the undercommons and not study, or whether the undercommons includes, or could include, non-instructional university service workers and forms of affective labor which are not immediately pedagogical

FRED: A lot of the questions from people on Facebook were, 'how do you enter into the undercommons?': well, you know, the 'undercommons' is a box, and if you open it you can enter into our world. A couple of people seem to be reticent about the term 'study,' but is there a way to be in the undercommons that isn't intellectual? Is there a way of being intellectual that isn't social? When I think about the way we use the term 'study,' I think we are committed to the idea that study is what you do with other people. It's talking and walking around with other people, working, dancing, suffering, some irreducible convergence of all three, held under the name of speculative practice. The notion of a rehearsal – being in a kind of workshop, playing in a band, in a jam session, or old men sitting on a porch, or people working together in a factory – there are these various modes of activity. The point of calling it 'study' is to mark that the incessant and irreversible intellectuality of these activities is already present. These activities aren't ennobled by the fact that we now say, "oh, if you did these things in a certain way, you could be said to be have been studying." To do these things is to be involved in a kind of common intellectual practice. What's important is to recognize that that has been the case – because that recognition allows you to access a whole, varied, alternative history of thought.

What I also want to say about that question is that it strikes me as being overly concerned with the rightness and legitimacy of the term. It's not so much that I want to say, 'oh, he or she didn't understand what we meant by study.' It's more like, 'okay, well, if that terms bothers you, you can use another term.' You can say, 'my understanding of study doesn't work for what it is that I think I want to get from what you guys are saying.' So, that person then has to have some kind of complicated paleonymic relation to that term. They have to situate themselves in some kind of appositional relation to that term; they have to take some of it, take something from it, and make their own way away from it. Insofar as you are now in what might be called a dissident relation, you are precisely involved in what it is that I think of as study.

So if the question is, 'does it have to include 'study?'", my first response is: okay, you don't understand what we mean by study. And then my second response is: but it's okay that you don't understand what we mean by study, because you're going to do something else now. So, my first response was to be correct and say, 'by study we mean this. The thing that I think that you want from what we're saying is precisely what it is that we mean by study.' And I'm gonna say, 'you seem to have a problem with study. How can you have a problem with study? If you truly understood what study is, you would know that it is this sort of sociality. That's all that it is.' But, then I would say, I'm being an asshole. That's sort of taking this guy to task for not having a properly reverent, adequate understanding of the term – and what I'm saying is that it's precisely his misunderstanding of, his active refusal to understand, the term that is an extension of study. Just keep pushing it. I will always think of his or her tendency to want to avoid or to disavow study as an act of study. But, if he or she doesn't think about it that way, that's okay.

STEFANO: At the same time, I'm happy for us to say more about *study*. I don't think it's a question of being completely passive about it and saying, 'do what you want.' There are reasons why we felt that we had to pursue these terms, and one of the key reasons – which Fred has already talked about – is our feeling that it was important to stress that study is already going on, including when you walk into a classroom and before you think you start a class, by the way. This is equally the case with planning. Think of the way we use *'policy,'* as something like thinking for others, both because you think others can't think and also because you somehow think that you can think, which is the other part of thinking that there's something wrong with someone else – thinking that you've fixed yourself somehow, and therefore that gives you the right to say someone else needs fixing. *Planning* is the opposite of that, it's to say, "look, it's not that people aren't thinking for themselves, acting for themselves together in concert in these different ways. It just appears that way for you because you've corrected yourself in this particular way in which they will always look wrong for you and where therefore you try to deploy policy against them." The very deployment of policy is the biggest symptom that there's something you're not getting in thinking that you need to do that – and it seems to me, really, the same with study. I think it's also fine for people not to use it or to find something else. But, equally, I think that the point about study is that intellectual life is already at work around us. When I think of study, I'm as likely to think about nurses in the smoking room as I am about the university. I mean it really doesn't have anything to do with the university to me, other than that, as Laura Harris says, the university is this incredible gathering of resources. So, when you're thinking, it's nice to have books.

FRED: Of course the smoking room is an incredible gathering of resources too.

STEFANO: Yes. So, I just don't think of study and the university with that kind of connection – even though originally we were writing about what we knew, and that's why the undercommons first came out in relationship to the university. I don't see the undercommons as having any necessary relationship to the university. And, given the fact that, to me, the undercommons is a kind of comportment or ongoing experiment with and as the *general antagonism*, a kind of way of being with others, it's almost impossible that it could be matched up with particular forms of institutional life. It would obviously be cut though in different kinds of ways and in different spaces and times.

FRED: Studying is not limited to the university. It's not held or contained within the university. Study has a relation to the university, but only insofar as the university is not necessarily excluded from the undercommons that it tries so hard to exclude.

STEVPHEN: The particular question you're responding to was asked by Zach Schwartz-Weinstein on the history of non-instructional academic labor, which brings me to what I wanted to ask. I understand there's a much broader and deeper understanding of study that you're working on. But, your work started in the 1990s by looking at particular conditions of academic labor. So this is a question about how the broader conception of study fits into the more specific conditions of academic labor you're talking about. You're talking about how certain kinds of academic labor pre-empt collectivity or, almost because they encourage a very individualistic investment in the labor, they pre-empt that sort of broader project from emerging. So, is this something that is very particular to academic labor or is this something that is more general to forms of labor that require this investment? I guess my question is: how do you understand the relation between the specific forms of class composition of academic labor and broader patterns? I think it's easy for the specific to be conflated with the more general kind.

FRED: When I think now about the question or problem of academic labor, I think about it in this way: that part of what I'm interested in is how the conditions of academic labor have become unconducive to study – how the conditions under which academic laborers labor actually preclude or prevent study, make study difficult if not impossible. When I was involved in labor organizing as a graduate student, with the Association of Graduate Student Employees at the University of California Berkeley I was frustrated with the way that sometimes graduate student investment in thinking about themselves as workers was predicated on the notion that workers don't study. But this was more than just a romanticisation of authentic work and a disavowal of our own 'inauthenticity' as workers. It was that our image of ourselves as academic laborers actually acceded to the ways in which the conditions of academic labor prevented study. We actually signed on to the prevention of study as a social activity even while we were engaging in, and enjoying, organizing as a social activity. It's like we were organizing for the right to more fully embed ourselves in isolation. It never felt like we studied (in) the way we organized, and we never approached a whole bunch of other modes of study that were either too much on the surface of, or too far underneath, the university. I think we never recognized that the most insidious, vicious, brutal aspect of the conditions of our labor was that it regulated and suppressed study.

STEFANO: Yes that was one side of what was bothering us. The other side of it was that it looked like the university – and the way that one worked in the university – was where study was supposed to happen. So, it meant that, on the one hand, you had some graduate students appearing to disavow study and, on the other hand, you had many academics who claimed to be monopolizing study or to be at the heart of study – and this for me meant that, first of all, study itself was becoming, as Fred says, almost impossible in the university. It was the one thing you couldn't do in the university not only because of people's vrious positions but also because of the administration of the university. But, secondly, it meant that it was impossible to recognize or acknowledge this incredible history of study that goes on beyond the university.

That said, probably there was something – I don't know about for Fred, but I needed to work through a little bit – that I was an academic worker and I needed to position myself in a way that moved beyond its restrictions. But the other thing was that there are certain ways in which that academic model of preventing study has been generalized. So, it's no longer just in the university that study is prevented. Because the one true knowledge transfer from the university has been its peculiar labor process. They successfully managed to transfer the academic labor process to the private firm, so that everybody thinks that they're an academic, everybody thinks that they're a student – so, these kind of twenty-four hour identities. People propose the model of the artist or entrepreneur but no, this is too individual, capitalism still has a labor process. The university is a kind of factory line, a kind of labor process perfect for reintroducing a version of absolute surplus value back into the work day by trying to fashion work into this model which we associate with the university. And when we look closely at what was really going on in the university, what was really transferred was everything but study, the whole labor regime and all the organizational algorithms dedicated to closing down study while performing intellectual work. So, the other reason to stay within the university is not just for a certain set of resources or because the teaching space is still relatively if unevenly open, and not just because somehow study still goes on in its undercommons, but because there is this peculiar labor process model there that's being exported, that's being generalized in so-called creative industries and other places, and which is deployed expertly against study. This is something Paolo Do has tracked in Asia where the expansion of the university means an expansion of this baleful labor process into society.

STEVPHEN: There's this argument put forth by the Precarious Workers Brigade and the Artworkers Coalition that what's interesting about artistic labor is not necessarily innate to itself but how it's a laboratory for a particular kind of extraction of value, which can then be generalized beyond the art sphere.

STEFANO: Yeah, exactly. I've learned a lot from them.

STEVPHEN: Connected to another point you make, when we start talking about "students as co-workers," would that be to sort of disavow the disavowal of study? In your previous writing on academic labor you talk about how academics cannot acknowledge their students as co-workers because this would pose a problem. So, what would it mean to acknowledge that co-laboring process, not just within the university itself but more generally?

STEFANO: I might not put that the same way today as we were putting it at that time. I felt like we were involved more in an internal critique around academic labor than I feel connected to now. It's not that I'd be running away from it, but I sort of felt we needed to do it so that we didn't feel like we needed to keep doing it. Instead of putting it that way, I might say, there's a kind of fear in the university around something like amateurism – immaturity, pre-maturity, not graduating, not being ready somehow – and the student represents that at certain moments. And supposedly our job with the student is to help them overcome this so they can get credits and graduate. Today it's sort of that moment that's more interesting to me, because that's a moment where your pre-maturity, your immaturity, your not-being-ready, is also kind of an openness to being affected by others, dispossessed and possessed by others. But, of course, in the university, what they're trying to do is get rid of that, so you can be a fully self-determined individual ready for work, or as Paolo Virno says, ready to display that you are ready for work. So, to me, it's less about the student as co-worker, though it's undoubtedly true that students do a lot of the work, and much more about the student, as Denise Ferreira da Silva would say, as an example of an affected body. And of course the professors, just like the philosophers that Denise is talking about, freak out at that student, while at the same time it's the thing they work on, it's a necessary point in the production cycle for them. They're trying to remove anything that feels like that kind of affection between bodies and to produce self-determined individuals. Entering with the student into that moment, at that affective level, is the part that interests me a bit more now than, say, engaging with them as the worker, though I don't think that's wrong. It just seems to me less than what could happen.

FRED: I think, looking back at those earlier pieces, that we just kept pushing ahead, and kept moving, but that the movement was predicated on us trying to think about where we were at the time. These are the conditions under which we live and operate, and we need to try to think about that. There's something wrong going on, let's think about how it is and why it is that things aren't the way we'd like them to be – and we just basically had the temerity to believe that our desire for some other mode of being in the world had to be connected to our attempt to understand the way that we were living and the conditions under which we were living at that moment. In other words, and to me this is a kind of crucial thing: I wasn't thinking about trying to help somebody. I wasn't thinking about the university as a kind of exalted place in which being there is a mark of a certain kind of privilege, and that the proper way to deal with or to acknowledge that privilege was to take this wisdom or to take these resources that I had access to and to try to distribute them in a more equitable way to the poor people who didn't have the relation to the university that we did. Me, I never thought about it that way. I was just always like: the university is fucked up. It's fucked up over here. Why is it fucked up? Why is it that shit ain't the way it should be here? Yeah, there's some stuff here, but obviously there's stuff in other places too. The point is: it's fucked up here, how can we think about it in a way to help us organize ourselves to make it better here? We were trying to understand this problematic of our own alienation from our capacity to study – the exploitation of our capacity to study that was manifest as a set of academic products. That's what we were trying to understand. And it struck us that this is what workers who are also thinkers have always been trying to understand. How come we can't be together and think together in a way that feels good, the way it should feel good? For most of our colleagues and students, however much you want to blur that distinction, that question is the hardest question to get people to consider. Everybody is pissed off all the time and feels bad, but very seldom do you enter into a conversation where people are going, "why is it that this doesn't feel good to us?" There are lots of people who are angry and who don't feel good, but it seems hard for people to ask, collectively, "why doesn't this feel good?" I love poetry, but why doesn't reading, thinking, and writing about poetry in this context feel good? To my mind, that's the question that we started trying to ask.

STEVPHEN: It's especially hard to ask that question in England where the assumption is that everyone's miserable and very polite about it anyways.

FRED: But, that's the insidious thing, this naturalisation of misery, the belief that intellectual work requires alienation and immobility and that the ensuing pain and nausea is a kind of badge of honor, a kind of stripe you can apply to your academic robe or something. Enjoyment is suspect, untrustworthy, a mark of illegitimate privilege or of some kind of sissified refusal to look squarely into the fucked-up face of things which is, evidently, only something you can do in isolation. It's just about not being cut off like that; to study the general antagonism from within the general antagonism. My favorite movie is *The Shoes of the Fisherman* and I want to be like this character in it named Father Telemond. He believed in the world. Like Deleuze. I believe in the world and want to be in it. I want to be in it all the way to the end of it because I believe in another world in the world and I want to be in *that*. And I plan to stay a believer, like Curtis Mayfield. But that's beyond me, and even beyond me and Stefano, and out into the world, the other thing, the other world, the joyful noise of the scattered, scatted eschaton, the undercommon refusal of the academy of misery.

STEFANO: About seven years ago I moved from the US to the UK, from a university system where graduate students taught on an industrial scale, to a more semi-feudal system with a lot of precarious adjuncts instead. But then I got connected with comrades suffering through the Baronial systems of Italy and elsewhere in Southern Europe, and if they wanted to study they had to leave the university, at least strategically. That opened up another question for me, which was when you leave the university to study, in what way do you have to continue to recognize that you're not leaving the place of study and making a new place, but entering a whole other world where study is already going on beyond the university? I felt I ought to have some way to be able to see that world, to feel that world, to sense it, and to enter into it, to join the study already going on in different informal ways, unforming, informing ways. When I speak about a speculative practice, something I learnt by working with the performance artist Valentina Desideri, I am speaking about walking through study, and not just studying by walking with others. A speculative practice is study in movement for me, to walk with others and to talk about ideas, but also what to eat, an old movie, a passing dog, or a new love, is also to speak in the midst of something, to interrupt the other kinds of study that might be going on, or might have just paused, that we pass through, that we may even been invited to join, this study across bodies, across space, across things, this is study as a speculative practice, when the situated practice of a seminar room or squatted space moves out to encounter study in general.

STEVPHEN: One thing that I asked Stefano last weekend, as I was reading the manuscript, is about the order of the chapters. Some of the pieces feel different when you change the order in which you read them, because you get a different sort of narrative arc, depending on where you start from and where you end up. I think part of what I'm realizing is that the project is less, say, "here's a coherent narrative that runs this way," but more sort of things which are put together and remain open and should be presented as sort of a collection that doesn't necessarily say, "our argument starts at one and ends at five." It's more of a collection of things which resonate with each other rather than having to develop sequentially.

STEFANO: Yeah, I feel that's true. What I think is that each one is a different way to get at a similar set of questions, to think about the general antagonism, to think about blackness, to think about the undercommons. I think the impulse for me and Fred is always to try and move towards the stuff that we like, and to move towards the mode of living that we like. We know that sometimes that involves moving through certain kinds of critique of what's holding us back. But, for me, each time, what's going on is that I'm trying to elaborate a different mode of living together with others, of being with others, not just with other people but with other things and other kinds of senses. At one point, for me anyway, I felt very strongly that this kind of policy world was emerging everywhere – and I wanted to talk with Fred about how to find our stuff again amidst all this kind of policy work in which everybody seemed from every spot at any moment to be making policy. I had this image in my head of a kind of return to a world in which every self-determined individual had the right to make brutal policy on the spot for every person who was not self-determined, which essentially is a colonial or slave situation – and the kind of ubiquity of policy, which all of a sudden, didn't emanate anymore just from government but from fucking policy shops in every university, and from independent policy shops, and from bloggers, etc. These policy people to me are like night riders. So, I felt at that moment it was necessary to deal with it in terms of, what would you say is going on that occasioned that kind of frenzied attack, this total mobilisation of the 'fixed'? What provoked this? That's why we ended up talking about planning. But there's also a part where Fred is very directly able to address blackness in a piece. So, we were able to start with something that we were feeling was an elaboration of our mode of living, our inherited black radical tradition. Then, that piece ends up with a kind of caution around governance.

At least from my point of view, I'm always approaching Fred, hanging out with Fred, to say, we know that there are things we like, so how can we elaborate them this time, not just for each other but also for other people, to say to others let's keep fighting, keep doing our thing. So, it's true that it isn't an argument that builds. To me, it's picking up different toys to see if we can get back to what we're really interested in. Not to say that that doesn't change. I have a richer understanding of social life than I did a few years ago. When I started working with Fred, social life, to me, had a lot to do with friendship, and it had a lot to do with refusal – refusal to do certain kinds of things. And then gradually I got more and more interested in this term, 'preservation,' where I started to think about, "well, refusal's something that we do because of them, what do we do because of ourselves?" Recently, I've started to think more about elaborations of care and love. So, my social world is getting bigger with our work. But, each piece for me is still another way to come at what we love and what's keeping us from what we love. So, it isn't in that sense a scientific investigation that starts at one end and finishes at the other end.

FRED: It's funny, this ubiquity of policy making, the constant deputisation of academic laborers into the apparatuses of police power. And they are like night riders, paddy rollers, everybody's on patrol, trying to capture the ones who are trying to get out – especially themselves, trying to capture their own fugitivity. That's actually the first place at which policy is directed. I think that a huge part of it has to do simply with, let's call it, a certain reduction of intellectual life – to reduce study into critique, and then at the same time, a really, really horrific, brutal reduction of critique to debunking, which operates under the general assumption that naturalised academic misery loves company in its isolation, like some kind of warped communal alienation in which people are tied together not by blood or a common language but by the bad feeling they compete over. And so, what ends up happening is you get a whole lot of people who, as Stefano was suggesting, spend a whole lot of time thinking about stuff that they don't want to do, thinking about stuff that they don't want to be, rather than beginning with, and acting out, what they want.

One of the people who wrote questions on Facebook is Dont Rhine who is part of a political/artistic collective called Ultra-red which I was lucky enough to be able to do something with a few weeks ago in New York. He was talking about the Mississippi Freedom Schools, and Ultra-red have been using the Freedom School curriculum as part of their performances. These are pedagogical performances. What they're engaged in is essentially a kind of mobile, itinerant practice of study that is situated around a certain set of protocols regarding the problematic and the possibilities of sound. What they're engaged in is this process which, to me, is totally interesting and a model for how one might be together with different people in the world, in different places. My point is that the Mississippi Freedom School curriculum asked a couple of questions of the people who were involved in it, both the students and the teachers. One question was: What do we not have that we need, what do we want or want to get? But the other question, which is, I think, prior to the first in some absolutely irreducible way, is what do we have that we want to keep? And of course there's a way of thinking about what was going on in Mississippi in 1964 that would be predicated on the notion that the last question you would ever consider to be relevant for people in that situation, for black folks in Mississippi in 1964, is what do they have that they want to keep? The presumption is that they were living a life of absolute deprivation – that they were nothing and had nothing, where nothing is understood in the standard way as signifying absence. What that second, but prior, question presupposes is (a) that they've got something that they want to keep, and (b) that not only do those people who were fucking them over not have everything, but that part of what we want to do is to organize ourselves around the principle that we don't want everything they have. Not only is a lot of the shit that they have bad, but so too is their very mode of having. We don't want that. We don't need that. We have to avoid that. And what I'm saying is that there is a kind of really sclerotic understanding of these problematics of having and not having, of privilege and under-privilege, that structures the university as a place where policy proliferates.

So, we began thinking about the university because we were there. And Stefano was saying, rightly I think, what we came to understand is that our attempt to understand the conditions under which we were working led us to recognize that those conditions were being farmed out, that those conditions were being proliferated all throughout the world – that the university was an *avant-garde* of policy making and a place where the ubiquity of policy was being modeled for other realms within the social world. And then, people were saying, "matter of fact, we can take a very sclerotic understanding of study, or let's say, of knowledge production and knowledge acquisition, and that can be the center around which we organize the export of this whole process and problematic of policy making." So that, yeah, now we'll model the workplace on a free school classroom. You won't have fixed, individual desks anymore. We'll have round tables and people can do something that kinda seems like moving around, and we'll say that we are concerned about your continuing education, and we want you to feel free to express ideas. What in fact people were doing was taking the kind of empty shell of what used to be called education and saying, "we can use this shell as a way of exporting the apparatus of policy all throughout the social world." We realized that not only are we trying to understand what's fucked up about our own situation, but we're trying to understand how it is that the essential conditions of our own situation are being exported everywhere.

STEFANO: Yeah, that's right. Policy is especially directed towards the poor, and one of the reasons for that is essentially because, as Fred was saying, the wealth of having without owning – which exists among the poor, which is not to say that the poor aren't also poor – the social principle of having without ownership is ambivalent. On the one hand, obviously, capital wants that; that's the whole intellectual property rights crap, of kind of keeping that stuff loose so people will be productive about it. But, on the other hand, it can't really be abided in the long term, and I think that's why you get this weird, what I call this extreme neoliberalism, where you get a back-and-forth, in which, one moment there are vicious kind of drones against the poor, these night riders making policy from anywhere said to be fixed against anyone said to need fixing, and then the next minute, governance is deployed against the poor. And it has to do with the alternatives to ownership that I think are an inheritance of the poor, or a disinheritance of it, or something. You know bad cop, bad cop.

I feel there's a relation between policy and governance that's at work here. Both of them get generated in the university – not the university alone, they also get generated in NGOs and other places as well. But, it strikes me that with policy what you're often dealing with is somebody whose presumption is that they know the problem. With governance you're dealing more with a situation in which they imagine in the first instance that, rather than having to fix someone in order to extract from them, there's the possibility of a kind of direct extraction, and this is also what the field of logistics desires. In this sense, governance reminds me of the way Mario Tronti talks about the labor process. Tronti doesn't use the term 'labor process,' but he says, "look, the worker brings everything: the class relation, antagonism, sociality. The only thing capital brings is the labor process, they set it up." As Poulantzas says, they initiate it and control it. It seems to me that this is what governance is. Governance is merely the labor process. It's the least of everything but it's the organizational moment, the organizational resistance to what we are doing. And it's because it's the organizational moment that we're in – a situation where, for people who are involved in forms of organization, like a teacher, for instance, that you are much more immediately confronted, because of policy and governance and their ubiquity, with either being almost immediately the police or finding some other way to be with others. You are much more immediately forced to choose. That seems to me, also, to give a sense of why there's so much anxiety in the university, almost immediately; there's no hiding in an imagined liberal institution anymore. In these kinds of algorithmic institutions where nothing but a logistics of efficiency operates, you're very quickly either the police when you work in the university or you have to find some other way of being in the university. I think that's because of the reaction to the growing forms of autonomy in social life, the reaction that takes the form of governance and policy. Academics are caught up in that. They have to confront the fact that there's no possibility that they can't choose sides.

STEVPHEN: I would ask then what other ways are there to respond to the seductiveness of governance? Or, what are your interests, what do you want? I'm thinking of the NGO world where you have this prospecting for immaterial labor, for interests in order to be governed. How do you find a response to that? The reason I look at it from the point of view of seductiveness is I know some of my friends, and myself, who have ended up in the academy or the NGO world because they were trying to avoid being drawn into a certain kind of labor process, so they thought of it as their escape. But, their escape just ended up being a different kind of prospecting, where they eventually got drawn into a different, almost deeper, more problematic form of labor.

STEFANO: Yeah, the meta-labor process that they got drawn into. The key thing with the NGOs – and this is to some extent true in the university, but not to the same degree, because of the strange figure of the teacher – the true ethos of the NGO is not to speak for a group that's not speaking, but to somehow provoke that group to speak for itself. It's all about, 'this group has to find its voice and speak up for itself against the dam, and this kind of thing.' On the one hand, you think, 'well, fuck, what else could you do? I mean, you've gotta fight the dam.' On the other hand, it does seem to me that you're asking people to call themselves into a certain form of identity. This is what Gayatri means by the first right being the right to refuse rights, I think. So, it seems to me that the NGO can often be a laboratory for trying to solicit from people, trying to prospect from people, certain ways that they have of being together, getting them to translate these for, ultimately, capital. I'm not a fan of this notion that we're going to be inscrutable or invisible to capital, or anything like that. But there are always elaborations of social life that are not comprehended or exploited by capital. Capital, in its agency, just doesn't get it, necessarily. Governance is a way to make it more legible to them in certain ways.

It's not because somebody is trying to be illegible. I think once you're trying to be illegible, you're already legible.

So, if you're asking me what to do in these kinds of circumstances, I agree it's a difficult question, and in practice I continue to teach in circumstances that also include some finishing of the student, giving them a mark and things like that. And I don't say that people should suddenly not do NGO work. But, I also feel that it's necessary for us to try to elaborate some other forms that don't take us through those political steps, that don't require becoming self-determining enough to have a voice and have interests – and to acknowledge that people don't need to have interests to be with each other. You don't have to start by saying, "I'm so-and-so, this is what I like to do." I mean, people don't have to relate to each other through fucking dating sites. You don't have to elaborate yourself as an individual to be with other people – and in fact it's a barrier to being with other people, as far as I can see.

FRED: I was thinking about something you said, Stefano, about how capital initiates, or provides a structure. And I wanted to say that I want to think a little bit more about this supposedly initiatory power that capital has. Because, I would say, what you're calling 'initiation,' is what I think of as 'calling the situation to order.'

STEFANO: Yeah, and then it flips a switch.

FRED: That's the way it works. And regarding the seductiveness of it, there are two ways to think about it. One is some kind of normative productivity that requires order, requires answering the call to order. Or another way to look at it would be that in order to be recognizable, you have to answer the call to order – and that the only genuine and authentic mode of living in the world is to be recognizable within the terms of order. But, it's kind of like that thing where you walk into class, you're the teacher and you get there a couple minutes early and there are people milling around and there's a conversation already going on, and some of them might be talking about stuff you might be talking about in class and some of them might be talking about something completely different – and at the same time, I've been thinking about something, either what we've been talking about in class or something completely different. My position, at that moment, what I am supposed to do is at a certain point become an instrument of governance. What I'm supposed to do is to call that class to order, which presupposes that there is no actual, already existing organization happening, that there's no study happening before I got there, that there was no study happening, no planning happening. I'm calling it to order, and then something can happen – then knowledge can be produced. That's the presumption.

It's very hard. What's totally interesting me is to just not call the class to order. And there's a way in which you can think about this literally as a simple gesture at the level of a certain kind of performative, dramatic mode. You're basically saying, let's just see what happens if I don't make that gesture of calling the class to order – just that little moment in which my tone of voice turns and becomes slightly more authoritative so that everyone will know that class has begun. What if I just say, 'well, we're here. Here we are now.' Instead of announcing that class has begun, just acknowledge that class began. It seems like a simple gesture and not very important. But I think it's really important. And I also think it's important to acknowledge how hard it is not to do that. In other words, how hard it would be, on a consistent basis, not to issue the call to order – but also to recognize how important it would be, how interesting it might be, what new kinds of things might emerge out of the capacity to refuse to issue the call to order. In recognizing all kinds of other shit that could happen, see what happens when you refuse at that moment to become an instrument of governance, seeing how a certain kind of discomfort will occur. I've had students who will issue the call, as if there's a power vacuum and somebody has to step in.

STEVPHEN: Like George Orwell being pressured to shoot the elephant.

FRED: I get so annoyed with a certain kind of discourse around that kind of weird narcissism – that double-edged coin of the narcissism of academic labor – in which you naturalise your misery on one side of the coin, and then on the other side of the coin, you completely accede to the notion of your absolute privilege. So, on the one hand, you wake up every day being miserable and saying, 'this is the way it is.' And on the other hand, you wake up every day saying, 'look how privileged I am to be here. And look at all the poor people who aren't privileged to be here.' One of the deleterious, negative effects of that particular kind of narcissism is that it doesn't acknowledge the ways in which one of the cool things about the university (I'm not saying this is the only place where this happens, but it is a place where this happens) is that every day that you go into your classroom, you have a chance not to issue the call to order, and then to see what happens. And the goddamn president of the university is not going to knock on your door talking about, 'how come you didn't issue the call to order?'

STEVPHEN: Well, the funny thing for me personally was my attempt to not be in charge in that sense and instead to try to start from the questions of "why are we here? What are we doing here?"… Let's say that in certain aspects they didn't get so well, namely, that the university's response was, "you're incompetent! We're gonna send you teacher training and show you how to issue calls to order."

FRED: And again I don't have the benefit that Stefano's had of being in both academic systems, but I know that in the US they don't come, the administration doesn't come to my class. What I think we have here is a situation in which the presumption that the necessity of the call to order is so powerful that they can pretty much count on people issuing it. But they don't have to check up on you. The presumption is that it's so absolutely necessary and indispensable so why would you do anything else? Which is great, because they don't check up on you. You can do something else. It's not that kind of surveillance and sort of worker discipline and regulation in the sense of it being an externally imposed force. The tricky thing is that the notion is that you are your own policy maker; you are your own police force. Hopefully, we will have trained you properly so that you will know you have to issue the call to order. At that point you have to police yourself.

What I'm really trying to say is, I think, it's important to make a distinction between the capacity of capital, or the administration, to initiate, as opposed to their power to call to order. There's a difference. They don't initiate anything. In other words, the call to order is not in fact an initiation. If it's an initiation, it's an initiation in the sense of being initiated into a fraternity. It's a new beginning, let's say. It's a moment of some sort of strange, monstrous re-birth. It's literally being born-again into policy, or into governance. But there was something going on before that. And that initiatory moment is double-edged. You are starting something new, but you are also trying, in a radical, kind of brutal way to put and end to something – and the horrible part is it's a moment of colonisation: you're putting something to an end and you're also trying at that very same moment to declare that it was never there. "Not only am I going to stop you from doing this shit, but I'm going to convince you that you were never doing it."

STEFANO: Yeah, that's right. So, it's sort of within that context that I think both of us pose the question that's important to us. In other circumstances, Fred and I have talked about this by thinking about a certain kind of song, a soul song that you might get in Curtis Mayfield or in Marvin Gaye, where something's going on, let's call it the experiment with/in the general antagonism, and then the song starts. You can hear the audience, you can hear the crowd, and then he begins to sing or music begins to start. So, the thing that I'm interested in is, without calling something to order, how can you still sing? In the sense that not calling something to order is different from saying that there's nothing that you want to do with others, there's nothing that you want to start with others. We have our own versions of insistence or persistence in study.

FRED: Form is not the eradication of the informal. Form is what emerges from the informal. So, the classic example of that kind of song that you're talking about, Stefano, is "What's Going On?" by Marvin Gaye – and of course the title is already letting you know: goddamn it, something's going on! This song emerges out of the fact that something already was going on. Then, from a certain limited perspective, we recognize, there are these people milling around and talking and greeting one another – and then, something that we recognize as music emerges from that. But then, if you think about it for half-a-damn-second, you say, "but the music was already playing." Music was already being made. So, what emerges is not music in some general way, as opposed to the non-musical. What emerges is a form, out of something that we call informality. The informal is not the absence of form. It's the thing that gives form. The informal is not formlessness. And what those folks are engaging in at the beginning of "What's Going On?" is study. Now, when Marvin Gaye starts singing, that's study too. It's not study that emerges out of the absence of study. It's an extension of study. And black popular music – I'm most familiar with things from the 1960s on – is just replete with that. That thing becomes something more than just what you would call a device – and it's also very much bound up with the notion of the live album. The point is that it's more than just a device. It's more than just a trope. It's almost like everybody has to, say, comb that moment into their recording practices, just to remind themselves, and to let you know, that this is where it is that music comes from. It didn't come from nowhere. If it came from nowhere, if it came from nothing, it is basically trying to let you know that you need a new theory of nothing and a new theory of nowhere.

STEFANO: Yeah, and this is also all over rap music, which is always about saying, 'this is where we live and here's this sound.'

FRED: I told you, "this is how we do it." My kids listen to some shit, and I'm trying not to be that way, but sometimes I'm like, "let me play y'all some good music." If you listen to the Staple Singers' "I'll Take You There," it's got one little chorus, one little four-line quatrain, and then the whole middle of the song is just Mavis Staples telling the band to start playing. "Little Davie [the bassist] we need you now." Then, her father, the great guitarist Roebuck 'Pops' Staples: she's like, "daddy, daddy." Then, the verse was like, "somebody, play your piano." That's the whole middle of the song. That's the heart of the song. Not the damn lyrics. It's her just saying, "play," and they're already playing. And that's not a call to order. It's an acknowledgement, and a celebration, of what was already happening.

STEVPHEN: Or you have James Brown saying, "take it to the bridge."

STEFANO: Yeah, and I think that's why, for me, I can't think in terms of a management of the common – because it seems like, to me, the first act of management is to imagine that what's informal or what's already going on requires some act to organize it, rather than to join it, rather than to find ways to experiment with this general antagonism. Also, I think that, for me, that's why, when we're talking about a kind of unsettling, what we're talking about is joining something that's already permanently unsettled, what's shipped, against what's being imposed on it. You're absolutely right because Poulantzas, when he's talking about initiation, all he's saying, basically, is, "it's 9am, turn the machines on." I mean, there's no way that could have been the beginning of anything meaningful, other than control.

STEVPHEN: When you talk about 'the prophetic organization,' how do you mean 'prophesy' or 'organization' there? If you're not just calling into being something that was not there, I'm trying to understand what the notion of prophetic would be in that sense. Is it calling into being that which is already in being?

STEFANO: For me, 'prophetic' and a lot of the terms that we're using are just forms for me to enrich being, so that it doesn't get flattened out into the way that it's understood so often in politics. For me, it's just a way to think about the already-existing enrichment of being, the already-social quality of time and space, which means that you can simultaneously be in more places, and be more than one, and that seeing things and hearing things is just a way of being with others. It means the standpoint of every standpoint and none as Fred and I say, the standpoint of the shipped, the *containerized*, the unsettled and unsettling.

FRED: What you just said seems right to me. It is definitely about seeing things and hearing things. It's funny, because I'm happily surprised that we used the term prophetic; I'm happy that's there now, because I associate that term so much with Cornel West. There were moments where I would have been pretty stridently against the use of that term, probably because of the association with pragmatism that West asserts. But now I'm like, that term's cool, because it is about seeing things and hearing things. Another way to put it would be: you talk about being able to be in two places at the same time, but also to be able to be two times in the same place. In other words, it's very much bound up with the Jamesian notion of the future in the present – and classically, the prophet has access to both of those. The prophet is the one who tells the brutal truth, who has the capacity to see the absolute brutality of the already-existing and to point it out and to tell that truth, but also to see the other way, to see what it could be. That double-sense, that double capacity: to see what's right in front of you and to see through that to what's up ahead of you. One of the ways in which academic labor has become sclerotic, let's say, is precisely because it imagines that the primary mode, specifically of a certain kind of left academic labor, is a kind of clear-eyed seeing of what's actually going on right now – and that the work is reducible to that. Or, another way to put it is that, insofar as that's what one conceives the work to be, one is only really doing the work when the work is absolutely in the absence of play, where play would be conceived of as pretending, as seeing what could be, as fantasy.

BEYOND & BELOW THE CALL TO ORDER

STEVPHEN: I'd like to follow up on the question of issuing a call to order, and more particularly about not issuing the call to order. Let's take the album *Nation Time* by Joe McPhee as an example. In one sense it seems very much that McPhee is issuing a call to order, haranguing the audience into a set piece of call and response: "What time is it?" "Nation time." But in another sense whatever order gets set up through that call to order, if it is one, then quickly breaks down or mutates into something else through collective improvisation. Fred, this connects closely to how you describe blackness as something happening "in the break" – but I was wondering how one could at the same time be calling to order and calling to mutation, or to a break, or perhaps to a different kind of order.

FRED: The enunciation, of "nation time," when Amiri Baraka first sang it, when McPhee echoes and riffs off and reconfigures it, is, I always thought, really a kind of announcement of the international and, beyond and by way of that, the anti-national. Black nationalism, as an extension of Pan-Africanism – which is resistance to a given Africa from within Africa accurately seen as a venal, administrative and accumulative combination of collection and division – cuts the nation, it seems to me. I mean, it makes sense, to me, only as this richly internally differentiated resistance to the Westphalian imposition, which comes fully into its own as the simultaneous invention and destruction of Africa, as the brutal interplay between colonial viciousness and the organization of racial murder on a grand scale. What gets called national struggle, how it shows up in cultural assertion, and what shows up as an international against national oppression and the imposition of parochial brutality, is what Fanon is after – to critique but also to destroy and disintegrate the ground on which the settler stands, the standpoint from which the violence of coloniality and racism emanates. I don't think we're just making this up. I mean, I think what we're gesturing towards is real – this phenomenon in which the appeal to the nation is an anti-nationalism, in which the call to order is, in fact, a call to disorder, to complete lysis. I mean this is what your question is getting at, Stevphen, and it seems to me that this is what we hear when we listen to that McPhee cut. And what's cool is the stridency and striation of his call and of the response to it. No purity of tone either in his horn or in his voice or in the voices of those who, for lack of a better term, respond; the soloist is already less and more than one and, like Cedric Robinson says in *The Terms of Order,* which is really this amazing and beautiful ode to disorder, the one who is said to have given the call is really an effect of a response that had anticipated him, that is the generative informality out of which his form emerges. They already know the answer to the question they sent him to ask. They already know what time it is and that combination of answer and question, that gathering in the break of all those already broken voices, is when music becomes a demand, takes the form of a demand, that shows up in the guise of a single voice or a national call. It's like a delirium (as Deleuze might say, by way of Hume) taking the form of, moving in the habit, putting on the habit, of a sovereign articulation, something that an "I" or a "we" would say. But what it is, really – what it is when people say shit like "What is it?" – is a relay of breath that comes from somewhere else, that seems like it comes out of nowhere. It's easy not just to get the origin wrong but to get the whole thing wrong by thinking about it in terms of an origin. I don't think McPhee is or means to be originary. Maybe there's some secret way, opened up by some unique and secret word, to move through this constant organization and disorganization of the demand that takes the form-in-deformation of a single voice consenting to and calling for its multiplication and division. That claim that Fanon makes about the demand being neurotic, in an already existing conception of psychological order or normalcy or whatever – and that's something that he says in *Black Skin* – is tied to the sort of recognition that an anti-colonial movement would necessarily be one that would tend toward complete disorder, total lysis. And the neurosis is tied, not just to the fact that from the standpoint of sovereignty, the demand for sovereignty's destruction makes no sense but also to the fact that the demand is spoken in his crazy language, in the crazy costume of the one who thinks he is the one. So the point is that the call to order is a call for and from disorder. That's where, I think, McPhee is coming from. If you listen you can hear where he's coming from.

STEFANO: For me, with regard to the occupation movement, there were three things in play at once, which you might call the request, the demand, and the call. The request is basically the stuff that Wendy Brown is herself always so paranoid about: that one is making a request to authority and by making a request to authority one is therefore already implicating oneself. Sure, there were occupation people for whom when people were saying 'demand' what they were really hearing was 'request' – request to someone – "we want you to reform banking, we want you to do this." Then, there's the demand, which is non-negotiable, which is I think what Kathi Weeks is interested in. But then, a minute ago, you were talking about a call, a call to disorder, which is already an enactment, an ontological enactment of something. So, the demand is uncompromising, but it's still in the realm of positing something that's not there, which is fine because there are indeed things that are not here. But I think the call, in the way I would understand it, the call, as in the call and response, the response is already there before the call goes out. You're already in something.

To me, the call is what these guys were trying to say when they said, "but these are biopolitical demands," or "this is a biopolitical politics," which is to say, it's neither a politics of requesting something from authority nor of demanding something despite authority. Rather some kind of demand was already being enacted, fulfilled in the call itself. I don't think that was totally clear to me or maybe to some occupy people – maybe to some it was scary when it was clear; it was certainly scary to authority when it was clear. And it was, of course, most clear not in the occupy movement but, for me, in the London riots, because the London riots, which – and Fred has written beautifully on them elsewhere and here we talk about them as irruptions – of logisticality, that which gives rise to the capitalist science of logistics, and today in rampant form." What's interesting about these riotsm, and I've talked to kids about it, after the three days, and they all said the same thing: "for three days we ran London. For three days London was ours. For three days it worked according to how we wanted it to work." And, basically, they didn't demand anything. They just started. There was a call: come out and let's just run the city for three days. Now, maybe they didn't run it exactly in the way everybody would have run it if the call was fuller or different. And, of course, those kids have all received incredibly ridiculous jail sentences and everything else. Occupy has been nothing compared to that in respect to vicious state repression in the court system. I mean, not to minimise some of the violence against occupy people in the US. The riots were really a place where you saw this kind of call. So, to me it's no surprise that the call through social media was what they criminalised most quickly.

FRED: I want to say something else about the demand. I still kinda want to hang on to that term. The reason I do is because, I certainly see the difference between request and call, I want to get back into the history of the word 'demand,' where it also means 'to make a claim,' and sometimes 'to make a legal claim' – and the whole notion of demand is that you speak with a kind of authority. The authority of the demand could be supplied by the state, insofar as you serve as an officer of the state, so that you have the state and its powers of violence and coercion behind you when you make the demand. But, there's also the notion of a claim or a demand in which the authority of the demand is from some kind of multiphonic delirium or fantasy that undermines the univocal authority of sovereignty. That's what I'm thinking of with regard to McPhee and his tone. You listen to that record. It's 1970. Coltrane died in '67, but he's still in the air everywhere. And his tone, which was a tone of appeal – 'appeal' is a cool word, 'appeal' as in to make an appeal but also peal; there was an urgent intensity to his sound, a stridency. So, what I'm trying to get at is there was this notion of the cacophony of the demand.

Folks who were basically saying "we don't want to make any demands" – there were two elements to it. One potential way of saying that we were resisting making the demand is to say that what we were really resisting was to make a request. We did not want to make a demand, because to make a demand is essentially to make a request, which is essentially then already to accede to the authority of the state to either grant or refuse your request, after the fact of having recognized your standing, your right to request, even though it is the source of your injury, even though your recognition by the state redoubles, rather than remedies, that injury. So, that's a kind of Wendy Brown formulation. Then, another version of it, I thought, had to do with the fact that the demand emerges from a certain kind of authority. The properly authorised and authoritative speech of a demand takes the form of a univocal, single speech. Essentially, a kind of sovereign speaker is now drowning out, or trying to collect within his own anthemic speech, all these other kinds of speech. So, again, some single, univocal notion of the demand emerges, when in fact what you've got is a whole bunch of people making a whole bunch of demands, some of which are contradictory – and we wanted to maintain that sort of ana(n)themic multiplicity, because that was the whole point.

What if authoritative speech is detached from the notion of a univocal speaker? What if authoritative speech is actually given in the multiplicity and the multivocality of the demand? This was something that was also happening at that same moment in the music, so that the figure of the soloist was being displaced. Even if the soloist was, in a certain sense, only temporarily occupying a certain kind of sovereign position, the return to collective improvisational practices was sort of saying, "we are making a music which is complex enough and rich enough so that when you listen to it you are hearing multiple voices, multiply formed voices. We are sort of displacing the centrality of the soloist." Or, another way to put it would be that, even within the figure of the soloist itself, there's this exhaustion and augmentation of the instrument, this tingling of the saxophone – and this is something that you hear in McPhee's playing on *Nation Time*. He was playing harmonics on the horn, so that the horn itself becomes something other than a single-line instrument; it becomes chordal, social. And that chordal playing shows up for us aurally as screams, as honks, as something that had been coded or denigrated as extra-musical – as noise rather than signal. So, what I'm trying to do is to consider this notion of the demand as an appeal, as a claim, where you're not appealing to the state but appealing to one another. An appeal, in this delivery – you're making all this sound, you're making all this noise. You're an ensemble, and that's bound up with that notion of study and sociality that we've been talking about.

So, I want to say that I agree with everything you say about the call, but I guess I want to maintain or keep that word 'demand,' just because of the particular way that Fanon indexes it, because he talks about it in relation to the settler's interested, regulative understanding of neurosis.

STEFANO: That part I like, but the part that I'm concerned with in Fanon is that the demand for him seems futuristic. And it seems to me that, when we were looking at the Panthers again, one of the things that seemed so cool about them is they had a revolutionary program that was partly about preservation. So, it was like a revolution in the present of already-existing black life.

FRED: Look, here's the thing: you're right. I like the fact that Fanon associates it with neurosis. In *Black Skin*, the neurotic is problematic – and it's, I think, very much tied to, or gesturing towards, a certain understanding of black sociality as pathological and there's nothing about that which Fanon wants to preserve, in *Black Skin*. In *Wretched of the Earth*, on the other hand, I think there's a lot about it that he wants to preserve. At the same time neurosis is also the condition of the sovereign, the habitual attempt to regulate the general, generative disorder. What does it mean to call for disorder in the sovereign's "native tongue?" How do you get to the ongoing evasion of natality which is where or what that call comes from or, more precisely, through? The path that is forged by negation and reversal doesn't get you there or gets you to someplace other than that, some delusion of origin or home, someplace available to or by way of a movement of return. I think Fanon is always trying to move against the grain of this itinerary of return, this reversal of image or standpoint. But that's why its so crucial to abide with the work of Cesaire or Baraka or Samuel Delany so that you can understand that the various returns they seem to enact or compose are always more and less than that. Fanon understands that the very taking of an anti-colonial stance looks crazy, from a normative perspective. For me, first of all, that's good. That's something that's worthwhile. In other words, what it's about is, "I'm gonna claim this thing that looks crazy from your perspective." But, of course, the problem, I think, with Fanon in *Black Skin*, is you can do this thing that looks crazy from the normative perspective, but of course in some complicated way there is no non-normative perspective. The non-normative is precisely the absence of a point of view, which is therefore why it can never be about preservation. Eventually, I believe, he comes to believe in the world, which is to say the other world, where we inhabit and maybe even cultivate this absence, this place which shows up here and now, in the sovereign's space and time, as absence, darkness, death, things which are not (as John Donne would say).

And what I want to do is say, against the grain of Fanon but in a way that he allows and requires me to say, no, let's look at this shit from our perspective, from the perspective of the ones who are relegated to the zone of the crazy or, to be more precise, I hope, from the absent perspective, or absence of perspective, of the delirious, the more and less than crazy. And what we're saying is we claim this, not just because it's against the grain of the normative, not just because it allows us to call for something in the future; we claim this because this is who we are and what we do right now. Now, Fanon doesn't say that in *Black Skin*, but I think he's approaching that by the time he gets cut off, basically. This is not simply to repress or forget the pitfalls of spontaneity or the problems of national consciousness; it is, precisely, to remember them and what sends them; to consider what moves at and in this interplay of study and an ever expanding sense of who and what we are. That Derridean 'who, we' is already active in Fanon's Algerian air – that open question of the human and its sound, which now we can take even further out into a general ecology or something like a Deleuzean 'plane of immanence.' And I think that you could project outward from Fanon's last work and then come back and get something out of that interplay of the neurotic and the demand that he is beginning to approach in the chapters on mental disorders and anti-colonial struggle in *Wretched of the Earth*, because he's recognizing that anti-colonial struggle is all bound up with the radical, sort of, non-normative form of cogitation, that it's gotta be, because it is, thought in another way. It's that shit that Shakespeare says: the lunatic, the lover, and the poet are of imagination all compact. Just edit it: the lunatic, the lover, and the anti-colonial guerilla, right?, are of imagination all compact. And that's an aesthetic formulation that Shakespeare's making. But it has massive social implications, which need to be drawn out, which in a certain sense Fanon is gesturing towards, something that we're associating with blackness and the undercommons, something he tries to reach, something we're trying to learn how to try to reach or reach for. But, what we understand as the social zone of blackness and the undercommons is the zone precisely in which you make that claim – so that the demand is a double-voiced thing, an enunciation in the interest of more than what it calls for. You are saying what you want, though what you want is more than what you say, at the same time that you are saying what you are while in the guise of what you are not. There's this other formulation of Baraka's that McPhee would have known as well: "The new black music is this: find the self, then kill it." That kinda thing gets said from the neurotic standpoint, in the neurotic habit, of the soloist. But the soloist is not one. Just like it was always about more than 'the right to vote' or the tastiness of the water that comes from this, as opposed to that, fountain.

STEFANO: And I think in part that's connected directly to being shipped, because it means that you unmoored from a standpoint. Once you're in all the circuits of capital, you're in every standpoint, and at that point, the demand becomes something of the future and the present, that has been realized and has yet to happen. So, it gets connected back up for me with what we were talking about earlier about hearing things and seeing things, and about the relationship between demand and prophecy, which again is totally bound up with having been shipped.

FRED: It's just like the stuff you were talking about: in another version of the shipped, of logisticality, Woody Guthrie is riding the blinds with folks who are one another's pillows. And you can segue from that immediately to "I ain't got no home anymore in this world." And you can segue from "I ain't got no home anymore in this world" to like Coltrane's *Ascension* or *Interstellar Space*, in which the musical form is all about the disruption, the making of new form, outside the notion of some kind of necessary structural return to a tonic. So, there's no tonal center. There's no home like that. The improvisations are unmoored in this way. And obviously this is also something that plays itself out in Arnold Schoenberg, or whatever. So, the point would be that, like, recognizing that the most adventurous and experimental aesthetics, where dissonance is emancipated, are hand-in-hand with the most fucked up, brutal, horrific experience of being simultaneously held and abandoned.

That double-edged logisticality, where the one who is shipped is also a smuggler, carrying something – and what he carries is, first and foremost, a kind of radical, non-locatability. The point is, there's a certain way of thinking about that impossibility of being located, of that exhaustion of location, that only can be understood as deprivation. So, like, by way of Frank Wilderson, who, when he elaborates his theory of the special antagonism that structures black life in the administered world also offers this brilliant articulation of this desire for home – "I don't want to be a cosmic hobo" – which is necessary to any possible embrace of homelessness. Woody Guthrie was a cosmic hobo, Coltrane was a cosmic hobo, so even if I could be something other than a cosmic hobo, I think what I'm gonna do is embrace homelessness for the possibilities that it bears, hard as that is, hard as they are. Homelessness is hard, no doubt about it. But, home is harder. And it's harder on you, and it's harder on every-god-damn-body else too. I ain't so concerned, necessarily, about the travails of the settler. The horrible difficulties that the settler imposes upon himself are not my first concern, though in the end they are a real thing. It's the general "imposition of severalty," to use Theodore Roosevelt's evil terms, that I'm trying to think about and undermine. He knew that possessive individualism – that the self-possessed individual, was as dangerous to Native Americans as a pox-infested blanket. Civilisation, or more precisely civil society, with all its transformative hostility, was mobilized in the service of extinction, of disappearance. The shit is genocidal. Fuck a home in this world, if you think you have one.

STEFANO: Just like the people we went to school with or maybe some of your Duke students or indeed settlers of the globe generally.

FRED: Yeah, well, the ones who happily claim and embrace their own sense of themselves as privileged ain't my primary concern. I don't worry about them first. But, I would love it if they got to the point where they had the capacity to worry about themselves. Because then maybe we could talk. That's like that Fred Hampton shit: he'd be like, "white power to white people. Black power to black people." What I think he meant is, "look: the problematic of coalition is that coalition isn't something that emerges so that you can come help me, a maneuver that always gets traced back to your own interests. The coalition emerges out of your recognition that it's fucked up for you, in the same way that we've already recognized that it's fucked up for us. I don't need your help. I just need you to recognize that this shit is killing you, too, however much more softly, you stupid motherfucker, you know?" But, that position in which you have no place, no home, that you're literally off center, off the track, unlocatable, I think it's important. Again, I think that there's something to be gained from that part of Fanon's double alignment of the demand with neurosis. It's sort of saying, basically, it's like Malcolm X, when he'd be talking about the distinction between the house negro and the field negro. And the primary distinction that he'd make was that the field negro would be saying, "where can I get a better job than this? Where can I get a better house than this?" He was claiming the location that really wasn't his, but what he was really claiming was the possibility of location. And Malcolm's like, "No! I'll be out in the field. Not only in the hope of something more, something other, than what you think you have but also because there's something in the field; that even in deprivation, there's an opening."

STEFANO: Yeah, I think that's also something I felt again in these London riots. It's always that stuff about, "why are they fucking up their own neighborhood?" Of course part of it is they don't own those neighborhoods. But part of it is also, like, "cuz there's gotta be something better than home."

FRED: It's like that, what did that Home Secretary say? What are the causes of the riots? She was like, 'shared criminality.'

STEFANO: She doesn't know how close she was to the truth.

FRED: She's ridiculous, and yet there's something deep and kind of true about that. I think you can make a good case that human being in the world is, and should be, sheer criminality. Which also, first and foremost, implies that making laws is a criminal activity.

STEFANO: The jurisgenerative stuff...

FRED: Those kids were, basically, like, "fuck this." And you're right, if you're implying that Occupy never got to that.

STEFANO: Yeah, it didn't get there.

FRED: A few people started talking about, "let's occupy everything. Let's occupy everywhere" – and that's more in line. But, "we won't come to your house and bother you." If that's the best you can do, then that's cool too. It's better to bother someone to death than to die. But we can move past that too.

STEVPHEN: One other thing I wanted to ask: I think part of the reticence about demands is also about a certain discomfort with thinking about or relating to the state, and how to relate to the state. I'm gonna ask two or three questions here, so it might be a bit of a mess. Not to get too caught up on definitions, I'm trying to understand the difference between how you understand the undercommons as opposed to, say, infrapolitics, or things coming out from people like Tiqqun, talking about zones of opacity. How does this notion compare, particularly in relation to thinking about the state? One of the things I've been trying to push you on for several years, Stefano, is your sort of knee-jerk reaction to someone like James Scott. You say "James Scott" and he starts kicking!

FRED: His knee hasn't jerked in twelve years! I'd love to see your knee jerk!

STEVPHEN: My question has something to do with his take on the state, and particularly that which cannot be taken into the state. So, in a book like *Seeing Like a State*, there are certain things which the state can't figure out. It can't figure out infrapolitics, it's completely incomprehensible to it. My suspicion is that you'd say, "no, that's stupid. Of course it's taken an understanding of infrapolitics. It does all the time." Which is why I want to ask you about the difference between undercommons and infrapolitics, in relation to the state. I'm guessing you are less reticent about the role of the state.

STEFANO: Well, it's not that I'm less reticent. I'm less convinced that there's a thing called the state, because I used to work in it. Okay, government and state are not the same thing, but I've never been able to understand the state except as an effect of certain kinds of labor. And, when I was involved with that kind of labor, there were all kinds of undercommons in the departments that I worked in. There was an underlabor. There was study going on all the time in government. And if government essentially produces effects of state in various ways, which seems to be what Tim Mitchell and some of the smarter guys around state theory think, then for me, it's not about being against or for the state, it's being about, as Tronti would say, within and against the state, but also with and for the undercommons of the state. So, I just don't line up on the side that there's a state, there's an economy, there's a society, even that there's state and capital in such a clear way. I have a much more, sort of, phenomenological, if I could use that word which I kind of hate, approach to the state. When you get close to it, there's all kinds of shit going on there. Most of it's bad. Most of the effects are bad. But, at the same time, some of the best study, some of the craziest undercommons people have been working in government agencies, local government agencies at the motor vehicle department.

I remember once going in; I remember me and my friend Pete, we tried to get a cover for *State Work*, my book about this stuff. We went into the big post office that they later closed in downtown Manhattan. It was in the days when the post office was just full of people actually working there, before the attacks of September 11, 2001 in New York. I went to the one in Durham very recently, actually, and it reminded me of what it used to be like in New York, before it was all securitized. It was only a few people but it was just like that: a big old post office. Everyone had their booth, and in lower Manhattan's post office behind almost every booth was a black or latina woman who had completely decorated the booth for heself. And it was full of, like, Mumia posters, pictures of kids, pictures of Michael Jackson, pictures of union stuff, everything. Every booth, so every time you went up, you got a different view. And I'm like, well, if these are the people who are supposed to be making an effect called the state, then, there's got to be an undercommons here too. So, it's not helpful for me to say I can do this and I will be invisible to the state. Or, I'm not making an appeal because the state will get me. That's not to say that the state won't throw me in jail or doesn't throw people in jail all the time. I just don't like to start from that position.

STEVPHEN: It sounds more like projecting sort of an accidental fetish character of the state that sees it as whole and coordinated and, of course, very sensible.

STEFANO: Yeah, and also, I think the fact that people work on an affective state – and there is a certain thing that goes on that doesn't maybe go on in private production, because you have some notion that you're producing the effect. Now, that's become more common everywhere else. So, there's been a kind of way in which, well, there used to be some idea that when you're working in productive industries you're producing stuff. Now of course everybody thinks they're producing effects everywhere they're working. So, also, it seems to me that a certain kind of distinction has broken down around that – and I think that's interesting. Also, I'm not against the production of effects. I don't think that it's bad that people should get together and imagine that they're producing something hard to see. It's just bad that they happen to imagine nation-states.

I guess that's my position on James Scott [laughs]. You know, I get enough shit for attacking James Scott. I really never give the guy a thought! I used to get criticised all the time when the *State Work* book came out, from my development studies friends because apparently I called him "an anti-communist," and that really made everybody berserk. But I just meant in the technical sense that he was against communism.

STEVPHEN: In the technical sense! [laughs]

FRED: I'm actually asking the question now, because I want you to say something more, Stefano, about this, because I actually think it's important. For Scott, what is it that he thinks he means by the state? Because what you're saying, Stefano, is that there's this monolithic thing that appears to be the referent when people utter the word 'state.' And you're saying it's not monolithic at all, and not only is it not a monolith but it's very, very thoroughly aerated. There are all kinds of little holes and tunnels and ditches and highways and byways *through the state* that are being produced and maintained constantly by the people who are also at the same time doing this labor that ends in the production *of the state*. So, what is it that these folks are producing? Scott seems to refer to a monolith that is unbroken by and in the very process of its construction. He's one of the ones who gets us back to the point where we ask, what is it that we don't like about that monolith. Well, its coercive power or its power to police or its power to make policy or to foster the making of policy or its power to govern or to foster governance and governmentality. So, what is he talking about? I give him credit, or I believe, however anti-communist he is, I believe he's sincere in his antipathy towards the monolith. To the extent that it exists, I hate it, too.

But, then, there are other people on the left who have no antipathy towards the state at all. And then I think they mean, it's not some sort of monolithic mode of existence that we are all captured by and contained within at the level of our own affective relations to one another and our everyday practices – because I think that's part of what Scott means. But what they're basically saying is, "no, what I'm interested in is this thing that has a certain kind of coercive power, and rather than that coercive power being granted to some other mug, I want it to be granted to me because I'll do the right thing with it. And also the main reason is I not only believe that I would do the right thing with it but I also believe that the kinds of things that I want to do at the level of scale can only be done by way of some sort of state or state apparatuses." So, their ploy is: "(a) I'll do it better and (b) I'm thinking about shit at the level of scale and you're just being silly and all you care about is these four people that you're talking to right now." See?

STEFANO: I do see, and I'm also interested in this question of scale, because that's the side of the argument scale ends up on and who it ends up on and with. But, one of the things I'm interested in, in the history of communism, let's say, is: under what circumstances could I allow myself to be taken up and possessed by others, be in the hands of others, give up anything like a kind of sovereign self-determination that I will vote on every decision, that I will oversee, that I will be like Lenin's inspectors, coming in to make sure the state's doing what it wants? What kind of communism could there be where I could just allow some people to do some shit for me, at the level of scale, and at the same time those people would also at other moments allow me to be doing that kind of thing? So, in what ways are we practicing, when we're for a dispossession of ourselves and allowing ourselves to be possessed in certain other ways, allowing ourselves to consent not to be one, at a moment that also lets people act on us and through us, and doesn't constantly require us re-constituting ourselves, which I think is implied? And this is, I think, the anti-communism of Scott. Scott's smallness is about self-determined autonomy. When you're small and in resistance, you're always in control.

Now, it's not that then instead we go for the state, because obviously the state, despite the fact that, as I say, it's not the thing he thinks it is, but a whole series of different kinds of shit – its effects are basically bad in the end. But, I'm interested in the way in which what we're doing already is and can be completely complex, that it doesn't require some other step and that we need to practice something else. Autonomists get this all the time in Europe: critics are like, 'oh, it's fine, you guys can go off and do that together, but we've got a hydro-electric system to run here.' And they often fall for that, and then sometimes you'll hear the autonomists saying, 'what would it mean to build autonomist institutions?' And maybe I misunderstood them but I think you don't need to build an autonomist institution. You need to elaborate the principle of autonomy in a way in which you become even less of yourself; or you overflow yourself more than what you're doing right now. You just need to do more of the shit that you're doing right now, and that will produce the scale. So, that's what's interesting to me. I'm interested in the way in which a deepening of autonomy is a deepening, not just among few people, not just that intensity which I value, but also it's a deepening of scale and the potentials of scale.

FRED: Yes, I agree. I bring up scale, not to denigrate scale, but to say, we can't cede scale to the people who assume that scale is inseparable from the state, or from what they mean by the state, which is a set of apparatuses and institutions which wield coercive power.

STEVPHEN: Agreed on that. Another thing I want to ask you about is, over the past few years there's been another revival or proliferation of kinds of alternative education projects, things like Edu-factory to free schools and all sorts of free universities. What they all were struck by is sort of, when you leave the institution, why do people want to imagine what they're doing in terms of the institution anyways? The limit of the conception of collectivity is another institution.

STEFANO: Yeah, I've been struggling with this myself, as I've been doing elaborations on a proposal for the School for Study that we're thinking about doing in France. The first three times I did it, I was putting in all kinds of shit that didn't really need to be there – that was a kind of recapitulation of the university in ways that didn't have to happen. It was only in the last version, really after Denise had looked at it and said, "why is all this other stuff in here? What you're really interested in is study, so why not just have it be a forum for study?" And that's when the name changed and that's when we began to click on what we were gonna try to do with it. And it's absolutely the case that, when you think you're exiting the university, you're not. You're taking all this shit with you.

But also, Matteo Mandarini gave us this very interesting phrase. Tronti has this phrase where he says, "I work within and against the institution." So, the Queen Mary project was this within and against the institution project. But it's also been elaborated in Precarious Ring stuff and other places as something that would also be known through co-research, something like "within and for." So, the within and against gets cut with a kind of within and for. When you move further out into an autonomous setting, where you get some free space and free time a little more easily, then, what you have to attend to is the shift, for me, between the within and against – which when you're deep in the institution you spend a lot of time on it – and the with and for. And that changes a lot of shit. All those things are always in play. When I say "with and for," I mean studying with people rather than teaching them, and when I say "for," I mean studying with people in service of a project, which in this case I think we could just say is more study. So, that with and for, the reason we move into more autonomous situations is that it grows, and we spend less time in the antagonism of within and against.

Some people love the productivity of the antagonism. Personally, I don't say it's not productive, but the further I get to the with and for, the happier I am. But that's a challenge, to remember that and to do it, and to learn how do it, if you spend a lot of time in the within and against, as we did. I'm only saying this to say, if I watch the migration of the Queen Mary collective project from the within and against towards the with and for that's available to us by becoming this kind of School for Study that we're talking about now, we have to study how to do that. We don't necessarily know how to do that, and we're still trying to figure out how to do that, because we've been inside so much. It's not that you ever leave the within and against – I don't care how far you squat. Obviously, there's a shift in what becomes possible and where you can put your attention in different circumstances.

STEVPHEN: Perhaps that's why the work both of you did of analyzing academic labor within a given position is necessary for the leaving, so when you leave you don't bring some of the things with you.

STEFANO: Well, at the personal level, and I started this morning saying this, and I still think it's true hours later, I had to go through that academic labor shit, especially with Fred, in order to free myself in a million different ways, including getting more into this autonomous stuff. I only feel now that that's had a full effect, that I can think free of all the shit that was in me through the labor process I was, and remain, immersed in. The first thing I made everyday when I went to university was myself, and the university these days is not necessarily the best place to make yourself.

FRED: I agree with that too. We were talking about how it was a way for us to understand who we were, and what was going on where we were – and to try to take more fully into account the necessity of understanding what your own conditions are. So, let's say that in some ways, the academic labor writings represented attempts at location and locating, mapping some sort of terrain that you were within. And I think the later stuff is much more interested in trying to achieve a kind of dislocation and a kind of dispersion – and, therefore, it claims a certain mobility. I agree with Stefano, well I don't know if we had to do that, but that's where we got started. We could have got started in another way.

STEFANO: Yeah, in a way, the undercommons is a kind of break piece, between locating ourselves and dislocating ourselves. What's so enduring for us about the undercommons concept is that's what it continues to do when it is encountered in new circumstances. People always say, "well, where the fuck is that." Even if you do that clever Marxist thing like, "oh it's not a place, it's a relation," people are like, "yeah, but where's the relation." It has a continuing effect as a dislocation, and it always makes people feel a little uncomfortable about the commons. For me it was like the first freight that we hopped.

FRED: Yeah, it's a dislocation. As our old friend Bubba Lopez would say, we started riding the blinds.

DEBT, CREDIT, AUTONOMY

STEVPHEN: Another area I wanted to ask about is your relationship to autonomism: How do you draw from post-workerism, in particular how it overlaps with the black radical tradition? Or more particularly the way that these overlaps and connections are passed over and ignored?

STEFANO: I'm not interested so much in the relationship where the debt would have to be credited, because increasingly for me I see the dominance of these two forms of debt in life, and they're both so baleful, they're both so moralistic. You know, as Marx said, debt is the moral judgment on the man. But also the other kind of debt, you know: I owe everything to my mother, I owe everything to my mentor. That stuff also becomes very quickly oppressive and very moralistic. There has to be a way in which there can be elaborations of unpayable debt that don't always return to an individualisation through the family or an individualisation through the wage laborer, but instead the debt becomes a principle of elaboration. And therefore it's not that you wouldn't owe people in something like an economy, or you wouldn't owe your mother, but that the word 'owe' would disappear and it would become some other word, it would be a more generative word.

I know that too many Italian autonomists never payed sufficient attention to the black radical tradition, and I know that that's continued up to the present to some extent. What I'm more interested in right now is the opportunity to place this vital strand of European experiment within a more global history. So, now certain autonomist stuff is sort of popping up in India. If it comes to India as if it came from Europe, as if it were an import rather than a version of something, then the first thing we're going to lose is an entire history, that I, for instance, don't know enough about, of autonomist thinking and movement in India, from India. So, it's not so much about giving credit to something, as it is of seeing this or that instance of something much broader. I'm not as interested in correcting genealogical lines, as I am in seeing European autonomism as an instance of something, and others can put it in whatever global context they want but for me it's an instance of the black radical tradition, an general inheritance of the shipped, the impossible tradition of those without tradition, an experimental social poesis.

STEVPHEN: I was sort of asking, not to say "oh well look what's missed, how bad it is that they've missed it," but more I'm intrigued by the particular ways of missing it. Autonomia seems to render blackness in a very Leninist way. So, we care about Detroit and nowhere else.

STEFANO: Yeah. Well, in that sense it also has an unfortunate tendency to reflect itself. Autonomia has a problem of vanguardism that it's always trying to get rid of. It stands against vanguardism, but it's always about, "who's really doing it and who's not really doing it?" It's still caught up with the idea that in order to be autonomous you need to be doing politics, and then there's the persistent risk of a definition of who's doing politics and who's not that's always at work. This is even in the Gambino pieces. For as good as they are, he's constantly looking for where DuBois or Malcolm X intersect with real politics, in my opinion. And yet as Matteo Pasquinelli points out, the impulse: "if difference, then resistance" is at the core of "Italian theory" and at is best this attention to what we would call the general antagonism is what this tradition shares with the impossible but actually existing tradition of black radical thought.

FRED: I defer to what Stefano said. I don't have that much to say about it. There's a very important, and let's call it righteous strain, of Afro-American and Afro-Diasporic studies that we could place under the rubric of debt collection. And it's basically like, "we did this and we did that, and you continue not to acknowledge it. You continue to mis-name it. You continue to violently misunderstand it. And I'm going to correct the record and collect this debt." And there's a political component to it, too. Maybe that's partly what the logic of reparations is about. Or even the "I have a Dream' speech, he's like 'we came here today to cash a check. A promise was given. We came to collect." That's what King said. So, I don't disavow that rhetoric or even that project. And, in many ways, I'm a beneficiary of that project, in ways that are totally undeniable and I don't want to deny.

I also think that that project is not the project of black radicalism – which is not about debt collection or reparation. It's about a complete overturning – again, as Fanon would say, and others have said. If that's your concern, if that's your project, the mechanisms of debt collection become less urgent. Or they become something that one is concerned about, but in a different way. Like, "I will note the debt, and I will note the brutal and venal and vicious way in which the debt is unacknowledged." When we talk about debt, to talk about the unpayability of debt is not to fail to acknowledge the debt. But, certain mugs just refuse even to acknowledge the debt. And I think a whole lot of what people want when they want reparations is in fact an acknowledgment, and they want an acknowledgement of the debt because it constitutes something like a form of recognition, and that becomes very problematic because the form of recognition that they want is within an already existing system. They want to be recognized by sovereignty as sovereign, in a certain sense. So, basically, I can read a big old book on the history of Western Marxism, and I can be alternatively pissed off about the way that its author can write that history without writing about CLR James. I'm alternatively pissed off, bemused, feel pity for his ignorant ass, whatever. You start to feel pity for his ignorant butt, but then you also understand the deep structural connections between ignorance and arrogance. And you can't feel sorry for an ignorant motherfucker if he's also an arrogant motherfucker, so then you get mad again. You stay mad, actually. But this is not a personal injury. You have to step to it in a different way.

So, basically, I'm with Stefano on this, which is that I feel like I want to be part of another project. Which is to say I'm not acceding to the fact; it's not like I'm just trying to turn my eye from it. I don't want to accept in silence without protest all the different forms of inequality and exploitation that emerge as a function of the theft and of the failure to acknowledge the debt. It's not just that I'm pissed off that Willie Dixon never got paid the way he was supposed to get paid for all them songs that Plant and Jimmy Page stole, but also that I want him or his locked-up grandson to get the damn money. I'm not sitting here saying, "I'm above them getting the money." I don't believe that what has happened in general is reparable, but if the United States finally decided to write me a check, I would cash the check and put it in the bank or go buy something stupid with it, a Rolls Royce or a Bentley, something that will really make George Stephanopoulos mad. I would accept the check, and be pissed off that it ain't as much as it should be. But I also know that what it is that is supposed to be repaired is irreparable. It can't be repaired. The only thing we can do is tear this shit down completely and build something new.

So, I'm interested in the autonomist tradition insofar as they've got something useful to say about the possibility and practicality of tearing shit up and building something new. My primary concern with it is not that they refuse to acknowledge this, although at the same time, their refusal to acknowledge other instances of a similar kind of thought, or a similar kind of social phenomena, does have a negative impact on the utility of what they do. So, that has to be taken into account as something that has material effects. But, in terms of just some desire for an acknowledgment, so that then Grace Lee or James Boggs or whoever, or the similar movements outside Detroit that some autonomists never really studied, can be noted... or, I think there's a kind of work that people want to do where it would be like, somebody might read George Lewis's book on AACM [Association for the Advancement of Creative Musicians] and say, "well, this has to be understood in a general framework that associates it with the autonomist movement," or something like that – and that would be an important, maybe, intellectual connection to make, and somebody could make it, and I think that would be cool. But, the bottom line is I think a whole lot of that kind of work of acknowledging a debt intellectually is really predicated on a notion that somehow the black radical tradition is ennobled when we say that the autonomists picked something up from it. It's as if that makes it more valuable, whereas it doesn't need to be ennobled by its connections to autonomist thought. Rather, what's at stake is the possibility of a general movement that then gets fostered when we recognize these two more or less independent irruptions of a certain kind of radical social action and thinking.

STEVPHEN: Thanks for that. The last thing I wanted to ask you, I think you've already started to answer in certain ways. At one point you write how "justice is only possible where debt never obliges, never demands, never equals credit... debts which aren't paid can't be paid." I was thinking about this, particularly in relation to the recent calls for debt abolition or a politics of debt that says, "no, we'll have to get rid of all of this debt." But to me it sounds like you have a sense of debt which can't be forgiven, can't be gotten rid of, and you wouldn't want to get rid of. So, I want to ask you, what's the relation between debt abolition and the debt that one would not want to get rid of?

STEFANO: For me, when I use the term 'abolition,' I mean it precisely in the opposite way. For me, abolition is both about a kind of acknowledgement that, as Fred says, there's no repairing or paying back the debt, so you couldn't really have anything like an abolition of debt. I mean, you could have debt forgiveness, but I would never use the term 'abolition' for that meaning. And, secondly, there's a whole history of debt that is not that history of debt, which doesn't need to be forgiven, but needs to become activated as a principle of social life. It can become, and already is in many instances activated as something which, precisely as something that doesn't resolve itself into creditor and debtor, allows us to say, "I don't really know where I start and where I end." This is even my point around the debt between a parent and a child. If it's really a debt, then that debt that you have is for more than you, it's not just for you, it passes through you, but it was a generative form of affect between two beings that is precisely valuable because it continues in certain kinds of ways. There's a whole history there, and what abolition means in that case is the abolition of something like credit or measurability or attribution, in a certain way.

FRED: I think this is where that distinction Stefano made between credit and debt is crucial. I think what people may mean, when they talk about the abolition of debt, is the abolition of credit. But they probably don't even really mean that. What they probably technically mean is forgiveness, which is to say, "we'll forgive this loan. Now, if you get in debt again, we're gonna want to get paid, goddamnit." Whereas, what Stefano is talking about, I think and I concur, is an abolition of credit, of the system of credit, which is to say, maybe it's an abolition of accounting. It says that when we start to talk about our common resources, when we talk about what Marx means by wealth – the division of it, the accumulation of it, the privatization of it, and the accounting of it – all of that shit should be abolished. I mean, you can't count how much we owe one another. It's not countable. It doesn't even work that way. Matter of fact, it's so radical that it probably destabilizes the very social form or idea of 'one another.' But, that's what Édouard Glissant is leading us towards when he talks about what it is "to consent not to be a single being." And if you think about it, it is a sort of filial and essentially a maternal relation. When I say 'maternal,' what I'm implying there is the possibility of a general socialisation of the maternal.

But, what's at stake, it's like, man, we went to look at this place yesterday, because I've got my whole commune plan. It's like ten acres, way out in the woods. And it's like a barn. The house is falling apart. I don't think we can do it. But there was this old lady. She and her husband, they built it how they wanted it to be. She was like, "I don't want to sell," but she's 91 and it's this kind of big old place, she can't keep up with it. People were telling us, "she owes her son a hundred thousand dollars." And me and Laura, driving back, we were like, "how you gonna owe your son a hundred thousand dollars? How do you owe a parent a hundred thousand dollars?" That's some crazy, barbaric shit. You have to be a barbaric monster to even be able to think of some shit like that. You know what? It's no more barbaric than owing Wells Fargo Bank a hundred thousand dollars. You think at first glance that it's barbaric because it appears to violate some sort of notion of filial, maternal relation. But, it's barbaric because it's a barbaric way of understanding our undercommon-ness. It's just particularly blatant because it's a relation between a mother and son. But, if it were a relation between me and Jamie Dimon, it's still barbaric. And that's the problem. So, the abolition of credit, the abolition of the entire way of looking at the world, which let's say we can place under the rubric of accounting, or accountability, or accountableness, or something, of calculation in that sense – the abolition of that, in a way that David Graeber thinks about it, but without any kind of sense of a return to some originary state of grace, but instead carrying all of what that history has imposed upon us. Hence this argument about where the autonomists got what they got... You know, I love C.L.R. James, but the shit that we now have under his name, was never his private property. Jazz ain't black people's private property. And that doesn't mean that musicians shouldn't get paid for what they do, within the context of this shit. What I'm really saying when I say that is: anybody who's breathing should have everything that they need and 93% of what they want – not by virtue of the fact that you work today, but by virtue of the fact that you are here.

What is it about adults that's so distasteful? You see a kid on the street or in your house, you know you're supposed to feed them, right? And then that same kid hits eighteen and all of a sudden you say, "I'm not feeding you." What's so vulgar and gross and smelly and distasteful about the average adult that you wouldn't just assume that he should get something to eat? I mean, you've gotta be sick to come up with something like that. I mean, who's the worst person in the world? Even he should have something to eat.

STEFANO: Given that, when you start to talk about this other kind of debt, you're talking about a history of aesthetics, a history of love, a history of organization, it's not merely about what you want to abolish – which is credit – but it's also about what you want to live in and how you want to live in it. And that's because the real debt, the big debt, the wealth that Marx is talking about, is precisely that: it's wealth. So, you want to figure out some way that that wealth can be enjoyed. And that's not by managing it, because managing it is the first step to accounting for it, attributing it or distributing it. It's about developing some way of being with each other, and of not thinking that that requires the mediation of politics. But, it requires elaboration, it requires improvisation, it requires a kind of rehearsal. It requires things. It's just that it doesn't require accounting or management. It requires study.

FRED: Man, I remember being little, being in Arkansas with my grandparents. My grandfather would give somebody a ride like 80 miles from our little town to another little town in his little 1969 green Buick Skylark. And there was this whole ritual process that would occur, and it had a couple of different parts to it. One part would be that somebody, my grandpa, would give you a ride, and before they'd get out of the car, the person would say, "how much do I owe you?" And he'd say, "nothin." Sometimes he'd feign a kind of, "why would you even ask me some shit like that?" They'd come a whole way just for a certain set of performances. "It don't mean nothin. Man, get out of this car," or something like that. But, if somebody got out of the car without asking that shit... He'd be like, "son, don't be like that." You have to acknowledge.

STEFANO: And you have to rehearse, because you're involved in the rehearsal of some other form of being in debt together. When we say that we don't want management, it doesn't mean we don't want anything, that it just sits there and everything's fine. There's something to be done, but it's performative, it's not managerial.

FRED: And the other part of it, which was just as important, was every once in awhile, if you're giving somebody a ride or if they gave you a ride, instead of asking how "much do I owe you?", you would just take some money out of your pocket and say, "put some gas in the car," and get out of the car. See the interplay between those two things. So, the reason why you asked somebody, "how much do I owe you?" is so that you could be engaged in this ritual process of basically disavowing the very idea of 'owe.'

STEFANO: Yeah, exactly. So that you begin to practice, improvise the relationship between necessity and freedom, not on the grounds of owing and credit, but on the grounds of unpayable debt.

FRED: Yep, most of the while, when you had some money, it wouldn't be a discussion. You would just say, "here put some gas in the car," and get out, leaving some money on the seat.

STEFANO: There's a necessity moment in it, but it's in the context of the freedom, rather than the other way around, and this is the only way it could be when we think of ability and need freed of the standpoint and then this is not a distributional politics anymore but an experiment in letting yourself discover new needs in your abilities and new abilities in your needs in the rhythm of, not against, the general antagonism, performed between the two and amongst the many.

FRED: Yeah, and this is why, for me, see I was looking at that, and it was illogical, if you want to call it that, but it was also performative. For me, I'm not saying that's the only form that study takes, but any notion of study that doesn't acknowledge that form of it is not the study that I'm interested in.

STEFANO: Where you find the abolition of credit you find study. But you can't call for the abolition of credit like you hear calls for the abolition of debt because the call to abolish credit is already always going all, it is a call that enacts, that is enacted. In other words, we don't need anything to get in debt together. We have already a superabundance of mutual debt we don't want pay, we don't want to pay, so what why would we call for anything? But we can join in this plenitude and its everyday performance. Moreover by joining perhaps we avoid some of what credit brings and what calls for debt forgiveness bring as unwanted results, from uplift to settlement.

FRED: Yeah, I mean, I love Fanon, but blackness isn't some thing that he thought of in an apartment with the others who had just arrived at their homelessness or, deeper still, at some knowledge of it. Now, some folks say that blackness is best understood not as a specific set of practices in which the people who are called black engage, because we have to account for the people who are called black but who no longer, or never did, engage in those practices; rather, blackness, they argue, is a project carried out by people whom we call intellectuals insofar as they refute, by way of essentially Hegelian protocols, some essentially Hegelian relegation to the zone in which all one can do is to engage in that specific set of authentic practices which have become, finally, nothing other than a mark of deprivation. My response is, no, the thing about blackness is that it's broad enough and open enough to encompass, but without enclosing, all of those things – and to suggest that somehow intellectual life exists on some scale on the other side of the so-called authentic is problematic anyway. Because I figure that performances of a certain mode of sociality also already imply the ongoing production of the theory of sociality. I mean, I'm into that, just like I'm into horny old Socrates when he sees some beautiful young boys he just wants to get next to, and they say, "man, come to the palestra because we need to talk about friendship," and he's like, "oh yeah, I'll come." That's good too, that lysis that never seems to come to an end – total, complete, but in an unexplained or undecidable completion. What they talk about, that was good too. There's a bunch of different possible places from which one might approach a critique of the administered world, or some knowledge of the administered self, and one of them is Papa's skylark.

REFERENCES

On the concept of study, we would like to thank Marc Bousquet and the editors of *Polygraph: an international journal of culture & politics,* especially Michelle Koerner and Luka Arsenjuk, for an earlier conversation on the concept.

For the chapter on planning and policy, we would like to thank the organizers and participants of the of the 2012 Winter Sessions at the Performing Arts Forum in St Erme, France for discussions leading to revision of this piece, and especially Jan Ritsema and Marten Spångberg.

For the chapter on logistics, we would like to point readers to the groundbreaking work of Ned Rossiter and his colleagues on the Transit Labour project: www.transitlabour.asia.

POLITICS SURROUNDED

Michael Parenti, *Make-Believe Media: The Politics of Entertainment* (New York: St. Martin's Press, 1992).

BLACKNESS AND GOVERNANCE

Karl Marx, *Grundrisse: Foundations of the Critique of Political Economy.* trans. Martin Nicolaus (New York: Vintage, 1973) 488.

Harryette Mullen, "Runaway Tongue: Resistant Orality in Uncle Tom's Cabin, Our Nig, Incidents in the Life of a Slave Girl, and Beloved," in *The Culture of Sentiment: Race, Gender, and Sentimentality in Nineteenth-Century America,* ed. Shirley Samuels (New York: Oxford University Press, 1992).

On questions of blackness and style see Thelma Golden, *Freestyle* (New York: Studio Museum in Harlem, 2001) as well as its anticipatory rebuttal, Amiri Baraka & Fundi, *In Our Terribleness: Some Elements and Meaning in Black Style* (New York, Bobbs-Merrill, 1970).

Jacques Lacan, "The Mirror Stage as Formative of the Function of the I," *Écrits: A Selection*, trans. Alan Sheridan (New York: W. W. Norton & Company, 1977) 4 and Hussein Abdilahi Bulhan, *Frantz Fanon and the Psychology of Oppression* (New York: Plenum Press, 1985) 155-77.

Michel Foucault, *The History of Sexuality, Volume I: An Introduction.* trans. Robert Hurley (New York: Vintage Books, 1978) 143.

Kara Keeling, *The Witch's Flight: The Cinematic, The Black Femme, and the Image of Common Sense* (Durham: Duke University Press, 2007).

PLANNING AND POLICY

Cornel West, "Reconstructing the American Left: The Challenge of Jesse Jackson," in *Social Text* No. 11, 1984-1985, No. 11, p. 3-19.

Fred Moten, Black Op, *PMLA*, 123:5, 2008, 1743-1747.

For discussion of command as a term of economy see Toni Negri in *The Porcelain Workshop* (2008), and see Paolo Virno on opportunism in *A Grammar of the Multitude* (2006).

FANTASY IN THE HOLD

Omise'eke Natasha Tinsley 2008 "Black Atlantic, Queer Atlantic: queer imaginings of the middle passage" *GLQ* 14:2 3.

Sara Ahmed *Queer Phenomenology: orientations, objects, others* (Duke, 2007)

Sandro Mezzadra and Brett Neilson (2008) Border as Method, or, the Multiplication of Labour http://eipcp.net/transversal/0608/mezzadraneilson/en

MINOR COMPOSITIONS

As well as a multitude to come…